Teaching Literacy through Drama

This book provides teachers of children at Key Stages 1 and 2 with a much-needed source of exciting and creative drama-based activities, designed to improve literacy. As useful for the drama novice as for the busy literacy co-ordinator, these flexible activities are designed to help teachers meet National Literacy Strategy (NLS) and National Curriculum requirements, particularly those for speaking and listening. The book is divided into 3 parts:

- **Part 1** looks at literacy and the power of drama as a 'brain-friendly' medium for teaching and learning.
- **Part 2** contains 10 structured practical units of work, each based on a different story, poem, play or traditional tale or rhyme, and each linked directly to the requirements and objectives of the NLS and the QCA objectives for speaking and listening.
- **Part 3** contains photocopiable Literacy Support Sheets for teachers to use and adapt for their own classroom needs.

All units of work have been tried and tested by the authors, giving teachers a springboard from which to enhance and extend their literacy lessons, and engage the imaginations of their pupils. The book is also the ideal resource for student teachers.

Patrice Baldwin is an LEA Adviser for the Promotion of Arts in Schools and **Kate Fleming** is a Senior Lecturer in Drama and English education at the University of Brighton. Both authors are educational scriptwriters for the BBC.

Teaching Literacy through Drama

Creative approaches

Patrice Baldwin and Kate Fleming

Foreword by Jonothan Neelands

RoutledgeFalmer
Taylor & Francis Group
LONDON AND NEW YORK

First published 2003
by RoutledgeFarmer
2 Park Square, Milton Park, Abingdon, Oxon OX14 4RN

Simultaneously published in the USA and Canada
by RoutledgeFalmer
270 Madison Ave, New York, NY 10016

Reprinted 2004 (twice)

RoutledgeFalmer is an imprint of the Taylor & Francis Group

Typeset in Gill Sans by Exe Valley Dataset Ltd
Printed and bound in Great Britain by St Edmundsbury Press Ltd, Bury St Edmunds, Suffolk

British Library Cataloguing in Publication Data
A catalogue record for this book is available from the British Library

Library of Congress Cataloging in Publication Data
A catalog record for this book has been requested

ISBN 0-415-25578-3

Contents

Acknowledgements

The authors would like to thank Nigel Nicholds for his continuous support and help with the completion of this book. They would also like to thank National Drama for bringing them together.

The authors are grateful for permission to reproduce the following material:

Unit 2: Illustration from *Katie Morag and the Two Grandmothers,* copyright Mairi Hedderwick, reproduced by permission of the author.

Unit 3: Illustration from *Voices in the Park*, copyright Anthony Browne, reproduced by arrangement with Transworld Publishers, a division of the Random House Group Ltd.

Unit 4: Text from *The Last Wolf*, copyright Ann Turnbull (1995), reproduced by permission of David Higham Associates.

Unit 5: Text from *The Man Who Sold his Shadow*, copyright Michael Rosen, reprinted by permission of PFD on behalf of Michael Rosen. Illustration from *The Man Who Sold his Shadow*, copyright Reg Cartwright, by permission of the illustrator.

Unit 6: Text from *Mufaro's Beautiful Daughters*, retold by John Steptoe, reproduced by permission of the John Steptoe Literary Trust and the Executors of the Estate of John Steptoe.

Unit 8: Painting, *The Lady of Shalott*, by John William Waterhouse, copyright Tate, London. Reproduced by permission of Tate Enterprises. Illustration, by Charles Keeping, from *The Lady of Shalott*, reproduced by permission of Oxford University Press.

Foreword

The introduction of the National Literacy Strategy has spawned a number of publications that seek to provide accessible ways for teachers to enrich their literacy work with drama. In some cases, such books tend to adopt a simplistic view both of literacy and of the profound learning opportunities offered by drama. This book breaks the mould. It is written by two teachers with extensive personal experience of teaching both literacy and drama.

The ideas and structures in the book are based on a thorough and often critical understanding of the important pedagogical connections between literacy and drama. The book goes beyond giving advice on the 'delivery' of narrow objectives; it seeks to challenge and extend the quality and depth of learning both in drama and in literacy. Patrice and Kate have ensured that the contents of this book represent the cutting-edge both of theory and practice in drama and literacy and their approach is firmly underpinned by the findings of research in both fields and research into how we learn and how we learn differently.

The book is in three parts. In the first, the authors offer a very clear rationale for the drama/literacy connection. At the heart of this connection is a view of language which is rooted in the world, in the ways that language is actually used for real life purposes, motives and intentions. Language, in all its variety, is approached through the imagined and physical contexts of drama worlds in which children can concretely explore the mysteries of human communication. Through working in dramatic contexts the child is offered the opportunity to use language as it is used in real life rather than being constrained to the artificial and abstract registers of the classroom. In acquiring language, young learners are also offered opportunities to learn more about themselves, others who are different and the worlds, in which they live and grow.

This section will be useful to teachers in a number of ways. It provides a grounding in key understandings and principles, which will guide teachers in their practice and planning. It offers a very useful set of arguments and justifications for drama, which will be of value to teachers who need to advocate the importance of drama in their staffrooms. Part I will also give confidence to teachers whose desire is to teach beyond the standards and levels of accountability; it encourages and endorses creative, intellectually challenging and relevant teaching strategies.

Part 2 is a rich anthology of structures and schemes of work, which connect drama and literacy for children from Foundation Stage to the beginnings of Key Stage 3. These are carefully wrought designs based on experience, based on tried and tested ideas, and based in a belief in children's powers of imagination. The authors offer a high degree of support for inexperienced teachers and a diversity of creative tasks for children. Opportunities for meaningful writing, discussion and artwork are signposted throughout the schemes. The selection of resources is challenging, fresh and exciting but it is also based on what is available to teachers in their schools.

Part 3 offers a further level of support by reproducing key texts and worksheets linked to the schemes for teachers to photocopy.

Patrice and Kate have written this book with love. Their own energy, excitement and enthusiasm permeates the pages and gives a welcome inspiration to those who know that there must be 'something more' than the dull drills and decontextualised exercises sometimes associated with the introduction of literacy strategies. Becoming literate, leading literate lives, are vital and essential goals for all children, but this book proves that the journey to literacy can be practical, enjoyable and challenging. I recommend it to you!

Jonothan Neelands
Senior Lecturer in Drama Education
Institute of Education
University of Warwick
May 2002

Part 1

Literacy, Learning and Drama

Introduction

This book aims to make literacy teaching an exciting and creative experience for both teachers and learners, whilst meeting National Curriculum and National Literacy Strategy (NLS) requirements. All the units of work have been tried and tested with children, teachers and trainee teachers. The units of work offered within this book are not intended as a complete drama curriculum or a complete literacy curriculum, but as a teacher's resource.

> *. . . it would be of value to many schools to have access to materials, ideas and strategies in the imaginative implementation of these strategies.* (DfEE 1999: 79)

Many teachers lack confidence and expertise to plan drama-centred literacy units of work, even though they see the need for them. This is partly due to the lack of professional development opportunities and limited initial teacher education opportunities for this in recent years.

The structured units of work within this book are based upon the NLS range of required texts and use the drama activities, most commonly specified within the statutory English curriculum. The learning objectives for each unit are primarily taken from the NLS teaching objectives and from the Qualifications and Curriculum Authority (QCA) publication *Teaching Speaking and Listening in Key Stages 1 and 2* (QCA 1999).

This book is in three sections. Part 1 gives the theory underpinning the practical use of process drama as a teaching and learning medium. It links it explicitly and contextually with current national strategies and curriculum requirements. It also links drama most importantly with the way recent research suggests children think and learn.

Part 2 contains a series of practical units which are linked directly to the requirements of the NLS. Each unit is planned to meet some of the requirements of the NLS for different year groups through the choice of text and the main teaching objectives. Additional objectives are drawn from those for speaking and listening published by the QCA in *Teaching Speaking and Listening in Key Stages 1 and 2* (QCA 1999). Linked drama objectives are also made explicit. Each unit therefore is intended to provide a series of practical activities that link and integrate teaching and learning in multi-sensory 'brain friendly' ways, whilst meeting curriculum requirements.

Part 3 contains worksheets which can be photocopied and which extend and develop children's thinking in relation to specific activities within the units as well as reflectively consolidating their learning.

Each unit contains a wide range of drama strategies and activities, which enable teachers to select those most appropriate to their own teaching situation and purpose. Text-based activities are provided for children to create, perform and respond to moving and still images, sound and speech. Contextualised writing opportunities are devised from within and in parallel to the unfolding drama. Teachers can revisit these units, selecting different activities to support their teaching or repeat those successfully tried with other texts of their own choice.

Many teachers are concerned that the demands of the primary school curriculum have restricted the time they are able to give to the Arts and creativity in children's education. Approaches to the curriculum, which offer opportunities for both children and teachers to be creative are essential in providing rich, meaningful, and engaging learning environments. In many cases teachers feel that they have had inadequate training to meet this challenge, but it is possible for all practitioners to meet the current requirements and teach well, without losing opportunities for developing creativity and the Arts.

Indeed creative opportunities are embedded within the values, aims and purposes of the National Curriculum.

> *... the curriculum should enable pupils to think creatively ... It should give them an opportunity to become creative.* (DfEE/QCA 1999a: 11)

Education is now beginning to take account of recent research into the way the brain works and the ways in which children learn and to relate this to the teaching and learning of today's curriculum. The result is likely to be an increase in creative and multi-sensory approaches to teaching, linked to clearly defined learning objectives, which is what this book aims to provide.

> *We see great value in integrating the objectives of high standards of literacy with those of high standards of creative achievement and cultural experience.* (DfEE 1999: 79)

Many learners may require an emphasis on some Arts-based approaches and methodologies. Children have a range of preferred learning styles and it raises interesting equal opportunities and inclusion issues about curriculum access, if subjects are taught in a way that repeatedly disadvantage a certain gender or type of learner. With such emphasis on verbal and written learning, teachers could be alienating children rather than incorporating and involving them. Learning objectives are now well defined in all subjects and teachers need to be seeking the most learner friendly and effective way of realising them.

Starting from a realistic acceptance that the literacy objectives and the time-tabled Literacy Hour remain fixed, there is still opportunity for creative teaching and learning through the Arts within the Literacy Hour and beyond. Drama, dance, music and art, all offer ways for children to respond to and express their individual and shared understanding of a text in ways that give opportunity for an energised, yet reflective, individual, group and class-collective response. Children need forms through which to explore and respond to text socially, emotionally, physically, morally, spiritually, culturally and cognitively. They need the opportunity to access text and express their developing understanding of texts, through art forms, involving the use and creation of visual images, movement and sound. Drama as a multi-sensory medium can provide an experiential structure for exploring text visually, auditorily and kinaesthetically. Its participatory nature motivates and promotes effective emotional learning, which is the most easily remembered learning, whilst at the same time providing intellectual stimulus.

> *OFSTED data on pupil response to learning indicates drama to be at the very top in motivating learning. (John Hertrich, HMI, OFSTED's Senior English HMI speaking at the NW Drama 3–8 Conference in January 1999* (DfEE 1999: 77))

Exploring texts through drama has long been accepted as a potent and successful teaching methodology. The imaginative framework drama provides, enables children to develop active, interactive and reflective relationships with the text whilst giving teachers the freedom to facilitate depth of learning in a diverse and exciting way.

The requirements of the National Curriculum for English are clearly defined and the framework of the NLS demanding. Catering for the diversity of children's learning and meeting these demands requires a creative and imaginative approach. Within both documents drama is both explicit and implicit. In the National Curriculum for English it is explicit as a strand of Speaking and Listening. It is implicit in all strands, i.e. Speaking, Listening, group discussion and interaction and Drama itself. Drama also spans the attainment targets of Reading and Writing, through its direct links with texts and playscripts. In the NLS, drama is again both explicit and implicit, within text level teaching objectives. Through drama, aspects of both sets of requirements can be easily integrated, enriching each other, and providing genuine and meaningful contexts for spoken, written and read language.

Participation in text level work through drama activities creates a sense of shared ownership through which children can investigate and develop characters, fill the gaps left in the text, reveal the subtext, and use their imaginations to bridge the divide between writer and reader, integrating and encompassing all aspects of literacy. Reading, writing, speaking and listening are interrelated activities and should be taught as such.

> *Teaching should ensure that work in speaking and listening, reading and writing is integrated.* (DfEE/QCA 1999b)

Drama can actively integrate these aspects of English contributing to the broader concept of literacy which balances the focus between understanding and the development of skills.

Drama is a shared and co-operative activity which fires the individual and collective imagination. This can be channelled into forms of artistic expression, which may be written or spoken, individually or collectively expressed. Drama can provide these forms through which children's personal and interpersonal collective responses to literature can be explored and communicated. Its multi-sensory nature provides flexible structures to facilitate the abstracting, constructing, reconstructing and communicating of meaning. The mind, body and emotions are given opportunities to connect and function together rather than separately, enabling children to make all-round and interconnecting sense of their experiences and learning.

Drama and Imaginative Role-Play at the Foundation Stage

1

The genesis of drama is in imaginative, dramatic play, and whilst this is evident throughout all the key stages, it is at the foundation stage that it is most apparent and prevalent. Indeed dramatic play is a natural developmental stage for children. Reluctance to play is usually an indicator of problems in other areas of development.

For children to be able to enter drama activities effectively they will need to already be able to play dramatically, to understand the notion of a make-believe world and to be able to communicate with others actively and verbally within that fictitious world. They will already, within their dramatic play, understand that objects can be used to represent other objects (e.g. a building block can be a piece of cake), and that it is possible to pretend that an object exists purely through mime. Once play moves beyond its initial solitary phase, parallel play alongside other children leads to interactive play with another child and negotiation develops. There is a point at which the child sees value in foregoing solitary play and compromising, in order to benefit from what other children or adults can bring to their own dramatic play (see Figure 1.1).

It is widely accepted that the pre-school child learns from the opportunity to role-play in imagined situations. In make-believe or dramatic play children are abstracting from their knowledge of the real world in order to establish for themselves a make-believe world within which they are empowered to operate and interact effectively. Much of their dramatic play involves re-enactment of the known and familiar. It remains important that young children entering the realms of the foundation stage and, later, the National Curriculum, do not lose the opportunity to play dramatically. Astute teachers, who are trained in the use of drama strategies will use dramatic play as a learning medium with which to deliver the curriculum. Furthermore, the elements of dramatic play and the unique imaginative framework, will remain ever present as drama lessons become a legitimised and educational 'play' forum. When a child is able to operate in abstract and imagined play-worlds with other children, the time is ripe for teachers and other empathetic adults to move in alongside the children, with a clear learning agenda. Adults can act as models for the pretending process and demonstrate how language, gesture and action can be appropriately used to explore and open up a variety of situations.

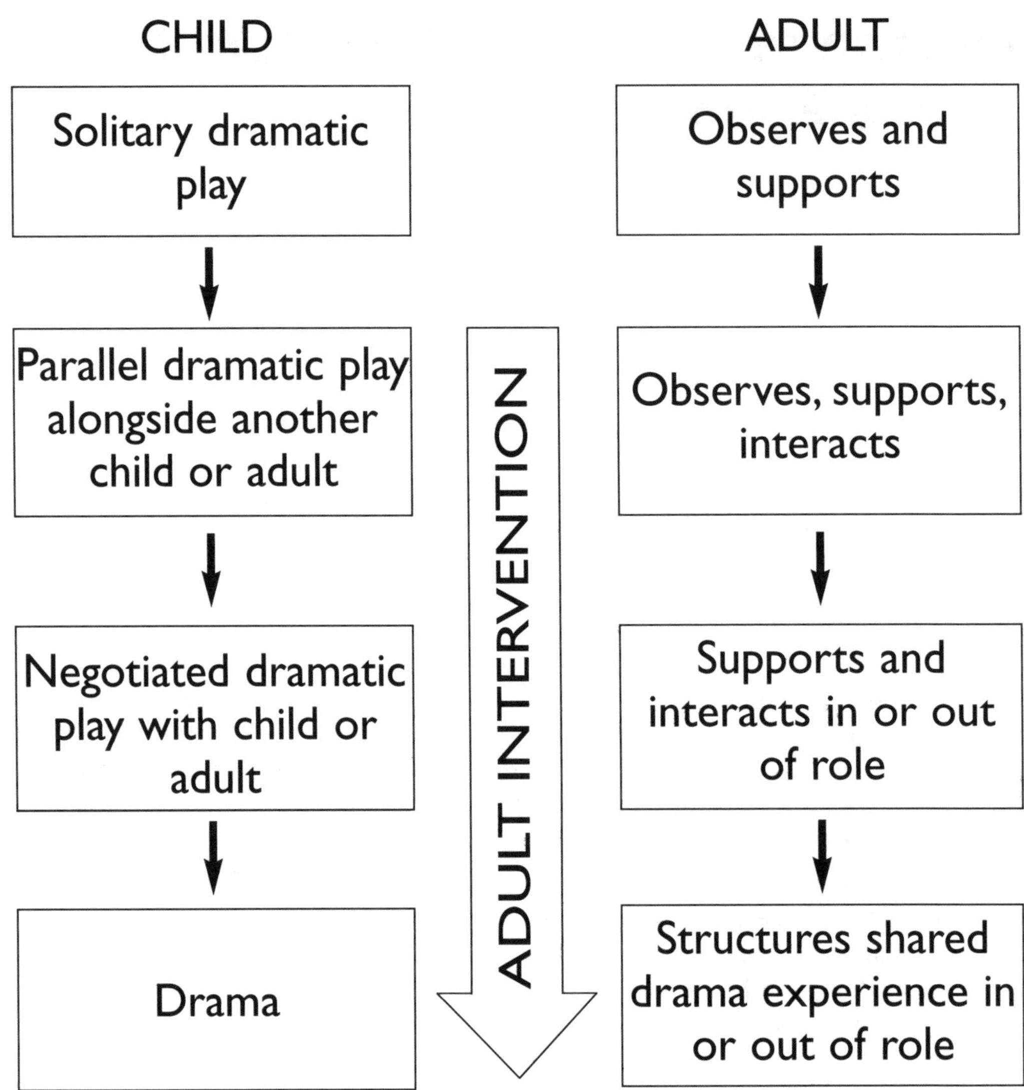

Figure 1.1 Opportunities for adult intervention in dramatic play.

As well as developing drama skills within the context of dramatic play, children are also involved in the conscious and subconscious learning of social rules, which apply to both dramatic play and drama. If teachers are introducing drama for the first time to young children, they may ask the children what is necessary for make-believe play to be successful with other children. What they say in response can be used as the rules of, or contract for, drama (e.g. 'we will support each other to make the drama work').

The role-play area provides children with the opportunity to experiment with ideas from the real world in an imaginary setting. They can assume different roles both familiar and unfamiliar, use appropriate language and gesture and begin to develop their ability to empathise. They can enjoy the flimsy border separating fantasy and reality and may move easily between the two, although it is important that they are helped to understand that there is a distinction between the real and imagined world and they need to know in which world they are operating. The role-play area stimulates and encourages a creative response to situations, developing original and independent thinking, opening up avenues for expression, and the chance to pursue their learning in a multi-sensory environment.

Early literacy skills, laying the foundations for the broader concept of literacy, can thrive in the imaginative play area. There is a strong element of story-making and re-enacting within children's dramatic play, which is fundamental to story-drama and the future development of literacy. Structuring the play to achieve learning outcomes, and providing reading and writing materials in imaginary contexts, supports and promotes a literate, imaginative environment (e.g. the hospital corner may have a notepad by the phone to take messages). This allows the children to make connections between speaking, listening, reading and writing and begin to understand their purpose as conveyors of meaning. Within the safety of the imaginative setting, they gain in confidence and are helped to prepare and become ready for the more formal aspects of literacy.

The Curriculum Guidance for the Foundation Stage (DfEE/QCA 2000), is organised into six areas of learning and drama can make a significant contribution in all areas.

- personal, social and emotional development
- communication, language and literacy
- mathematical development
- knowledge and understanding of the world
- physical development
- creative development

Each area of learning within the guidance has listed opportunities that practitioners, including teachers, should acknowledge. Drama and role-play as a creative teaching and learning medium can be linked directly with, and across, all six areas.

Drama as a medium for developing personal, social and emotional development:
• is an inclusive, social, group activity that invites emotional engagement; • helps give the child a sense of their identity as part of a group; • depends on mutual trust, support and respect in order to work effectively; • helps children to establish positive and mutually supportive relationships in small and large group situations; • is a context for empathetic and personal response to both children and adults who join in alongside them in role;

- uses classes as cultural microcosms within which children can explore the similarities and differences of human behaviour and learn about different types of relationships;
- uses the children's own ideas, allowing them to develop their own interests within the drama frame and in so doing can raise their self-esteem and self-image.

Drama as a medium for developing communication, language and literacy:

- provides powerful contexts for speaking and listening;
- values children's talk through enabling it, within a public class forum, to influence the open-ended direction of the drama;
- is a language-driven medium of communication, which can be based on narratives, nursery rhymes and songs;
- provides opportunities for the children to communicate their thoughts, ideas and feelings;
- integrates communication, language and literacy development within shared contexts;
- generates real opportunities for speaking and discussion in role as well as shared writing in role with the teacher as scribe;
- motivates children to extend their use of language and to try saying and doing things that are at the edge of their existing competencies;
- enables the teacher in role to offer language models in drama mode;
- gives opportunity for questioning characters, making statements and retelling their imagined experiences in and out of role;
- provides contextualised opportunities to ask, initiate, refuse and greet in role;
- provides a means of understanding symbolism and the juxtaposition of words and silence;
- involves the use and interpretation of verbal and non-verbal communication such as gesture, facial expression and body language to express feelings and meanings to others;
- requires children to respond to the communications of others;
- with the teacher in role, gives significant opportunities for the stimulation of interactive pupil response;
- is a forum for the teacher in role to act as a catalyst for communication;
- develops story-making originating in children's dramatic play and play is fundamental to the drama process; involves the creation of imaginary characters, settings and plots, building on these narratives by revisiting and retelling them, thus changing, adapting and developing their stories;

- can be a context for developing early literacy skills, laying the foundations for the broader concept of literacy;
- is teacher-structured play which uses the child's ability to play dramatically as a means of achieving learning outcomes;
- can provide engaging fictional contexts for introducing reading and writing materials;
- supports and promotes a literate imaginative environment which makes connections between reading and writing enabling children to begin to understand their real purpose to convey meaning;
- provides a safe imaginative setting through which children can gain in confidence before encountering the more formal literacy at Key Stage 1.

Drama as a medium for developing knowledge and understanding of the world:

- offers imaginary worlds within which children are supported to understand and make sense of the real world from within a distanced and safe context;
- provides distanced, powerful 'as if' experiences which encourage shared exploration, problem-solving and prediction and critical thinking;
- stimulates curiosity in children;
- can sharpen children's awareness of the real world and its cultural diversity;
- stimulates different ways of thinking about the real world;

Drama as a medium for mathematical development:

- can help develop mathematical understanding through enjoyable, engaging dramatic play and imagined drama contexts (e.g. shops);
- enables abstract concepts to be given a visual and tactile form;
- can provide reasons for thinking mathematically in role in order to use and apply mathematics in a powerful imaginary context, giving motivating reasons for finding solutions and problem-solving.

Drama as a medium for physical development:

- can generate ideas and develop concepts which can then be expressed through physical movement as an aesthetic art form;
- helps children to access, develop and consolidate ideas and concepts kinaesthetically through linking thought, action and movement;
- gives engaging and motivating contexts for responsive, controlled, devised and expressive movement individually and in groups.

Drama as a medium for creative development:
• provides a responsive multi-sensory learning environment within which children are able to go through a process of making connections, generating original ideas, solving problems together, playing with and expressing ideas and feelings through a variety of teacher-fashioned forms and representations; • stimulates curiosity, exploration and experimentation; • provides a safe forum and framework for risk-taking without failure, for playing together with the unexpected and unpredictable; • is a forum for constructing, deconstructing and recreating ideas with everybody's ideas valued and accepted; • encourages, values and fosters creativity, originality and multi-sensory expression; • provides opportunities to work creatively alongside adults as fellow artists who may function as supportive creative models and facilitators of the children's own creativity; • involves imitation but gives the opportunity for children to experience and experiment imaginatively with their imitations of real-life people and events; • is not about children re-enacting prescribed drama texts and stories with children simply enacting teachers own interpretations of materials and ideas through performance, as this does not necessarily make creative demands or provide creative opportunities for the children; • enables children as audience/participants to be guided by teachers to recognise and appreciate the aesthetic qualities of their work and the work of others; • involves the development of drama skills, knowledge and understanding to inform and enhance future creations.

Drama as a Creative Teaching and Learning Medium

2

The importance of creativity and its integral relationship with culture and education has become increasingly apparent throughout the last century. Once again educators are beginning to acknowledge that creativity and creative thinking are essential to the nation's future development and to meeting the educational challenges posed by our future workforce. This is documented clearly in *All Our Futures* which defines creativity as:

> *Imaginative activity fashioned so as to produce outcomes that are both original and of value*. (DfEE 1999: 29)

Drama fits easily within this definition, indeed it could almost be a definition of drama itself. Imaginative activity is one of the main characteristics of creativity and also the cornerstone of drama. It is logical therefore, to suppose that drama can provide children, through a variety of teacher-fashioned forms and representations, with a responsive multi-sensory learning environment, which is likely to facilitate rather than inhibit creativity. Within this environment, they are able to go through a process of making connections, generating original ideas, solving problems together and playing with ideas and feelings.

Drama provides agreed and open structures and forms through which children have opportunities to create, apply and express individual and shared imagination in a forum which supports risk taking without failure and the safe handling of the excitement of the new and unexpected. This imaginative framework motivates and stimulates curiosity, exploration and experimentation by encouraging the construction, deconstruction, generation and recreation of ideas, all of which are valued and considered by the teacher and peers. Children have the excitement of generating imaginative ideas that are original to them, are listened to by peers and teachers and may be used to shape the way the drama develops for the whole class. They are creatively empowered, alongside, and with their fellow creators.

Drama creates a shared focus and purpose for creative thought and action based on real-life experiences and imagination, which all children bring to the drama space. Whether the children are playing in the role-play area, spontaneously improvising in a drama lesson or presenting a staged theatre performance, by its dynamic, interactive and live nature, dramatic activity always generates shared, original and creative outcomes which are different every time and which offer a sense of individual and shared ownership.

Creative thinking is central to the drama process. In education it should involve teachers and children being free to make learning links between experience, knowledge, skills and present understanding using make-believe. Through drama they can gain new knowledge, develop and apply their skills and gain greater understanding, which in turn informs and enhances further creativity.

Drama provides a structure for interpreting, expressing and communicating, of giving concrete form to personal and collective creative thought. It focuses on children making meaning together through the potent fusion of real-life knowledge and imagined experience on an integrated active, affective and cognitive level and then expressing and communicating their understanding, in order to deepen and affect the understanding of others. Teachers can guide and support children both as participants and audience to appreciate the aesthetic aspects of their work and the work of their peers as well as that of creative professionals, such as theatre directors and playwrights. Ideally children will have opportunities to work creatively alongside adults as fellow artists, including actors and theatre-in-education teams, who may function as supportive creative models and facilitators of the children's own creativity.

Developing creativity is demanding and to a great extent relies on the teacher's own creativity, sense of challenge, and belief in the strengths and creative potential of each individual. It is important to encourage children to believe in their creativity and to foster an environment which raises self-esteem and confidence, and rates creativity as important within the learning process. When teachers are seen to value creativity it is more likely to be valued by the children themselves. A learning environment that values and fosters creativity should be a basic entitlement of every child, and every teacher should be enabled and encouraged to work creatively to meet the requirements placed upon them.

Creative and critical thinking skills are needed to generate and extend ideas and in the application of imagination. Taking children beyond what they already know requires not only the recognised skills of problem-solving, but the creative formulation of new problems and the discovery of new solutions and representations.

Drama as a teaching and learning medium that uses and develops multiple intelligences

Some teachers have found it helpful to consider the structuring and effectiveness of drama, with an awareness and understanding of Howard Gardner's theory of multiple intelligences. It is a useful model from which to consider planning for a multi-sensory and creative framework for teaching and learning. Gardner goes some way to making explicit what the good teacher already knows implicitly, that every child's brain is wired up differently and that they are each intelligent, in a multiplicity of ways. This results in all children having different preferred learning styles and profiles.

Howard Gardner has suggested that every learner possesses a multiplicity of intelligences, including linguistic, mathematical, spatial, kinaesthetic, musical, interpersonal and intrapersonal. The majority of teaching and learning is now utilising and developing mainly verbal intelligence, yet children think, learn and construct meaning for themselves in a variety of ways. Some children are predominately visual learners who respond most readily to the written word and visual images, whereas others are more auditorily orientated and the spoken word and sound has greater impact on their learning. There are children who are kinaesthetically orientated and respond best to learning through the sensation of movement and more tactile teaching approaches. To deprive children of a diversity of learning opportunities that allow them to apply a range of intelligences may be seen as limiting equality of learning opportunities and repeatedly disadvantaging some types of learner, often boys. Children need the opportunity to think, learn and demonstrate their knowledge, skills and understanding of drama and its content in a range of ways that are not restricted only to the written and spoken word and teachers need to consider this in their planning.

When planning drama it is worth considering whether the range of strategies, materials and resources used in a lesson or series of lessons are spanning multi-sensory and multi-intelligence learning (Table 2.1).

Table 2.1 Using and developing different intelligences through drama

Intelligence	**Means by which it might be used and developed**
Linguistic intelligence	Use of text, teacher in role, role-play, thought-tracking, improvisation
Logical/mathematical intelligence	Structuring movement activities and presenting logical image sequences
Visual and spatial intelligence	Creating and changing images, staging, movement, tableau
Bodily and kinaesthetic intelligence	Movement, dance-drama, improvisation, enactment, mime
Musical intelligence	Using and linking music and emotion within the drama context, creating soundtracks, sound collages
Interpersonal intelligence	Teacher in role, improvisation, group play-making, tableau, performance
Intrapersonal intelligence	Empathising and reflecting whilst working in role

Drama appeals to a wide range of learners as it invites them to access, understand, develop and communicate their learning creatively, in and across the whole curriculum, verbally, visually and kinaesthetically using and developing a wider range of intelligences than many other subjects.

The teacher has the responsibility to ensure that the child learns, regardless of what type of learner they are and this will mean approaching teaching and learning in a variety of ways. There is no point in trying to persistently teach a child in the same way if it is not working (e.g. if a child fails to understand imagery in a text when it has been verbally explained repeatedly, then teachers would be well advised to move into enabling the children to create the image, not just give even more verbal explanation). Thinking and sensitive teachers will change their approach and teaching strategies in order to accommodate the learner, and the drama teacher has the advantage of a powerful range of well-tried, yet sophisticated strategies that can be used to motivate a wide range of learners.

Drama and Literacy

3

The interrelationship between drama and literacy

Primary teachers spend a considerable amount of time teaching the NLS objectives for reading and writing but may not be meeting the full requirements of the statutory National Curriculum for English, which also includes explicit statutory requirements for speaking and listening. Since the introduction and implementation of the NLS, there has been less attention given to the planned development and teaching of speaking and listening, which includes drama. The teaching of drama is statutory, yet many schools claim difficulty in timetabling it in addition to the Literacy Hour. The high stake assessments in English are also focused on reading and writing and teachers are inclined to spend increasing amounts of time on what is to be assessed; indeed they are encouraged to do so. Yet speaking and listening is the cornerstone of communication, which is defined as a key skill by the National Curriculum. Its development should not be taken for granted or left to chance.

The Qualifications and Curriculum Authority published *Teaching Speaking and Listening in Key Stages 1 and 2* (following the introduction of the NLS and before the publication of National Curriculum 2000), to assist teachers in termly planning and delivery of speaking and listening. This publication can be used alongside the NLS framework to link termly teaching objectives as the basis of integrated blocks of work for reading writing, speaking and listening. This integrated 'block' approach enables schemes of work to be developed that include drama and can provide an integrated learning experience for children, rather than an atomised one. When the later Key Stage 3 literacy document was produced, drama was included as part of speaking and listening alongside reading and writing within the framework. Speaking and listening, reading and writing are interrelated and integral to the exploration of written and read text. Drama not only integrates the different strands of speaking and listening, but can also contextualise the teaching of reading and writing.

Drama provides a particularly powerful methodology for developing the teaching and learning of literacy in a broader sense. Definitions of literacy are now expanding across a myriad of social, intellectual and cultural contexts. It seems that the more narrowly literacy has been defined officially, the broader the range of literacies that have emerged in educational parlance; visual literacy, cultural literacy, computer literacy. Drama is itself multifaceted and can be used to develop children's expertise and understanding across a range of literacies. Literacy is not simply the ability to read and write, but encompasses all aspects of communication and understanding.

Drama gives structured literacy opportunities for pupils to respond:
• *socially* (working in and out of role together to create and communicate shared understandings and meanings); • *intellectually* (thinking in and out of role); • *physically* (enacting); • *emotionally* (feeling, personally responding and empathising, in and out of role); • *morally* (linking thought, action and consequence); • *spiritually* (enduring personal insights); • *culturally* (recognising and valuing diversity).

Drama as a context for speaking and listening

Children speak, listen and play dramatically and imaginatively, but speaking and listening skills still require and benefit from planned support, intervention and teaching. Children will not necessarily meet a broad range of situations in which they hear different types of speech for different purposes and are required to adapt their own speech according to audience, anymore than, without planning, they will have the opportunity to write, in a supported way, for a range of purposes. Teachers have a key role to play. They need to create engaging contexts for modelling and practising types of speech which are appropriate for the child developmentally and which span a range of purposes. Drama, rooted within speaking and listening, can provide, through imagined experience, an endless range of opportunities for integrating all aspects of English.

Drama is statutorily part of English because presumably it is seen as predominately a language-based art form. It is also a social art form, requiring children to work together to create their drama, which in turn may, through performance, be communicated to others as audience. This opportunity to share their drama, invites children to consider the dramatic role of language and the way in which it can be used to enhance the tension, atmosphere and focus on performances and the depiction of character. The interpretation and preparation of drama requires children to discuss, exchange ideas, sift and refine, accept the suggestions of others, co-operate and collaborate.

Drama activities such as role-playing and hot-seating create genuine contexts for language and reasons to communicate. Children are required by the drama to use language, which is appropriate to both role and situation, including different models of speech and registers. This enables them to experiment with vocabulary and syntax and to realise that language is dynamic, interactive and changing and can influence the ideas, attitudes and actions of others, both as participants and audience. In drama, contexts can be structured to give opportunities for children to speak as any person, in any devised situation, at any point in time or in any place. It engages children because it is living language, communication in the here and now. Drama is where language is applied and practised.

Drama as a context for reading

The relationship between drama and literature is close. Yet the NLS has little explicit reference to drama, other than drama texts which are reading and writing focused; playscripts, performance poetry, studying a Shakespeare play and devising scripts. Children must not receive these texts purely in terms of reading and writing. Study of these texts, which were written for performance, implies the need for a drama activity if they are to be taught effectively. Playwrights produce playscripts that are intended for performance, initiating a process which is intended for others to interpret and develop actively and interactively using movement, image and sound, as well as words.

A teacher with an understanding of drama methodology and form will be able to look at a range of texts other than drama texts and focus on the NLS text-level teaching objectives, using drama as a context for exploring, making meaning and investigating subtext and inference.

Good drama and good narrative poems and stories, like good plays, have narrative structures, characters, settings, plots and dilemmas to be resolved and problems to be solved. By helping children, through drama, to enter a fictional setting actively, to take on roles and empathise with characters, they can develop their ability to look beyond the words, to access underlying meaning, and to create their own meaning. Structuring activities which focus on key moments enables children to make deductions, relate ideas to their experience and make connections between new knowledge and what they already know. Fully competent readers need to engage emotionally with the text, and the critical awareness of the broad concept of literacy is enhanced and enriched through the interactive relationship that drama and text generates. Good authors use the way in which language can be ambiguous, subtle and rich in metaphor. By creating multilayered texts, they leave gaps for the reader to fill, inviting individual responses to make the text complete and original. Drama can be used to fill these gaps, by looking at what has been left out as well as re-enacting what is on the page. This can contribute to a sense of co-authorship of the text and collaboration with the author.

The NLS text-level work lays emphasis on progressively developing children's understanding of the narrative structure of character, setting and plot.

Setting

Within the drama experience children have structures provided. These structures enable them to actively create their own shared fictional worlds and to enter the many fictional worlds that have been created already by authors for them as readers. Authors introduce and develop settings for their readers which they are intended to imagine and hold in their mind's eye, just as drama teachers create dramatic landscapes. Using words the author builds up descriptions and visual images of fictional settings which drama can help children transfer into concrete images and settings within which they can then interact.

Character

Authors develop believable characters and, through drama, teachers support the children to become or interact with those characters. The characters are embedded in the text and the children, as enactors and performers, are motivated to delve deeply into the text to support their portrayals and enactments of characters and situations. An author invites the reader to enter the fictional world of their story, playscript or poem cognitively and emotionally. A drama teacher takes the author's character and makes it explicit through structured exploration and enactment. The children, as both readers and participants, enter the written worlds actively and collectively and are supported and invited to engage emotionally not only *with* the characters but *as* the characters. Empathetically, through drama, they are guided to appreciate and understand different character's viewpoints and feelings at different points in the story. They can voice the thoughts and feelings of characters at key points from within the text and, as participating readers, they are open to the challenge of their peers both as audience and participant, if they behave out of character at the expense of the shared drama experience. This is a significant motivator for children to read and analyse the text in order to 'get the character right', research the character, and discover more for their interpretation within the public arena of drama.

Plot

The author has to create an engaging plot in order to keep the reader reading. The drama teacher can recreate with the children, and hold in time, the key moments in that plot, enabling the children to live through, experience and reflect on the key or pivotal moments that the author has constructed and presented.

When children read a text, they are primarily invited to apply their linguistic intelligence to the task. This may be easier for girls than boys as the linguistic domain is one in which girls perform better. Different types of learner may respond differently to the same text. The same written words can evoke different responses in differently orientated learners. Visual learners for example may be more drawn to the visual imagery within the text. More kinaesthetic learners may be more drawn towards the action elements. Taking the words and exploring them verbally, visually and kinaesthetically enables children to access the written text using a wider range of intelligences and learning styles. The children may all be readers but they will not all experience and respond to the same text in the same way. In drama, the teacher has the opportunity to support the children as readers to understand the text through their senses in a multiplicity of ways.

If we acknowledge that children as readers can be supported to understand text more fully through employing a range of multi-intelligence, multi-sensory strategies, which drama is uniquely placed to provide, then we need to look at the world of reading as it is for children in our schools and to see where drama can profitably fit into this. One key area which needs to be considered is the reading SATs. With a curriculum driven by assessment, it is important that children are helped to perform well in 'child friendly' ways. The test experience needs to be bridged closely with good preceding practice.

Drama as a context for writing

Improving writing standards is an identified area of development for many schools, particularly for boys. The NLS makes many challenging demands on the young writer, and drama can be a strong support in providing meaningful contexts that stimulate and motivate children to write, both in and out of role, within and outside of the drama, individually and collectively. Drama provides a shared, experiential, structured experience through which enactment can precede and help formulate writing of all kinds. Children can be given a reason to write in role in the first person or from another's point of view for an imagined audience (Figure 3.1).

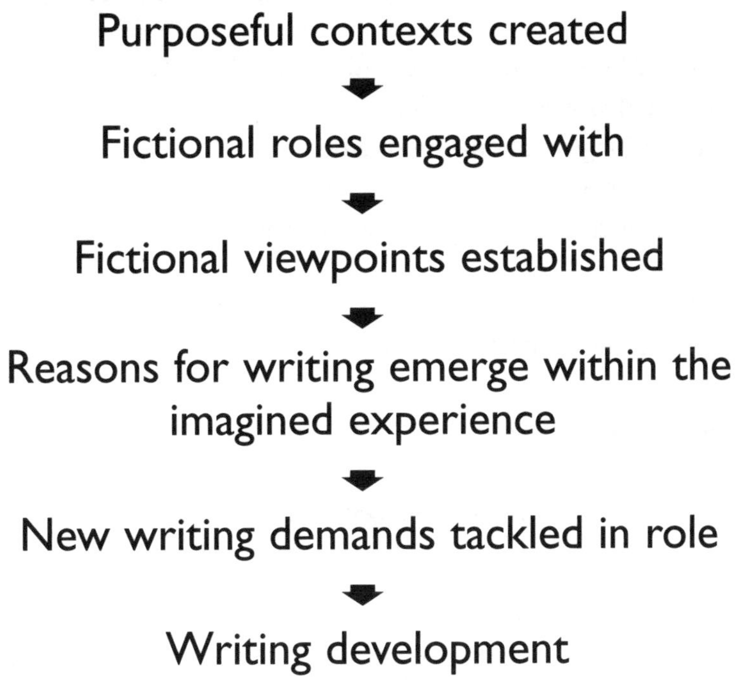

Purposeful contexts created

↓

Fictional roles engaged with

↓

Fictional viewpoints established

↓

Reasons for writing emerge within the imagined experience

↓

New writing demands tackled in role

↓

Writing development

Figure 3.1 Writing through drama.

The effect of writing on others lies behind its purpose and effectiveness. Drama offers an engaging context within which children use spoken or written language with the purpose of affecting others. The teacher and other class members are a receptive audience, as they themselves have invested emotionally as co-participants in the same drama (Table 3.1). With the drama as a forum the writer in role can elicit immediate audience response to their written word and can experience first-hand the effect and power of their written word on others within the drama form.

As drama creates a genuine context for the exploration of text to raise children's literary awareness, it simultaneously creates an exciting context for writing. With writing, as with reading, it is necessary for children to engage emotionally to be effective creative writers. This cannot be achieved by simply learning a set of rules. Writing is subjective and reflective, and the role of the teacher is crucial to the process. Providing instruction in basic skills is not enough, children need stimulation and something to write about. Drama is able to motivate children's imaginative thinking and give them the confidence to embark on what for many children can be an arduous and stressful task. It enhances the opportunities to write with purpose by placing children within the text, giving them the imaginative ideas and the willingness to commit themselves to the permanence of the written word.

Drama provides opportunities for:
• creating and expressing kinaesthetically, visually and/or verbally before moving to the written word; • writing individually or collectively from within a role during or after the drama; • writing from different viewpoints as different characters; • shared and guided writing in role; • empathetic writing/emotional engagement; • a range of imagined purposes for writing; • audience motivation for shaping writing due to the study of the effect on audience/participants; • a range of imagined writing audiences who can respond in role to the writing; • actively linking and crossing genres; • actively generating shared texts/scripts which then become part of the drama; • reflecting on 'lived' enacted experience through writing.

The nature of drama can furnish children with the ideas and imaginative experience to fulfil the demands of writing alternative sequels, using story structure to write about their own experience, writing openings and ends to stories, thinking about tension, suspense, atmosphere and scene setting. To be able to discuss and become familiar with different genres of writing can ease the technical difficulties required to annotate, construct playscripts, extend verses for performance poetry and compose additional scenes to existing plays.

Table 3.1 What children need as writers

CONTEXT	Drama provides shared imagined contexts in which children as writers are supported by peers and teachers as co-participants.
STRUCTURE	Drama provides characters, settings and plots.
CONTENT	The spoken word and imagined experience becomes the writer's first draft.
PURPOSE/BRIEF	Drama can provide reasons for writing which are integral to the development or understanding of the drama. Drama creates opportunities for imagined briefs within 'real' contexts.
IMAGINED AUDIENCE	The teacher and class are predisposed to respond with shared understandings and experiences. Audience response is evident and emotionally linked, informing and becoming integral to the drama.
WRITING SKILLS	These need to be at a level that do not hamper the writing process at the creative process stage. Drama can give in role possibilities for the use of scribes or shared writing using several children's collective writing skills.
ACCESS TO A RANGE OF GENRES	Drama provides a range of fictional contexts which link readily to different genres of writing (see Table 3.2). It can also provide models of genres as texts used within the drama or with the teacher modelling writing in role. Writing may be shared or guided in role by peers or teachers.
CONFIDENCE AND SELF ESTEEM	Children can be treated as writers in the drama (mantle of the expert) and thus see themselves as writers in their own and others' eyes. Their writing is valued in the drama and this raises self-esteem which can transfer beyond the drama.
TIME	The writer needs time in which to work through the writing process. Extended writing is more likely to take place outside the drama activity or lesson but short pieces of writing that synthesise and are given meaning laden through the drama experience can be short (word, sentence, phrase) and can be developed within the drama time.
REWARD	Intrinsic or extrinsic reward is required to maintain motivation. This reward may be peer audience/participant response or the reward of the child's writing influencing and shaping the action (ownership/co-author of storyline).

Drama strategies as a writing framework

Specific drama strategies can be selected and adapted as a way of planning and shaping different types of individual, shared and guided writing. When considering the range of drama strategies available to the teacher alongside the range of writing that is required by the NLS, certain drama strategies link readily to support specific types of writing. These links are exemplified in Table 3.2:

Table 3.2 How drama strategies and activities can function as writing frames

Text type	Supporting drama strategy	Drama activity	Example unit / drama activity reference in Part 2
Picture storybooks Wall story Captions for pictures Class book	Freeze-frame Tableau Still Image	First the children agree with the teacher the key moments in the class drama-story. Different groups create different still images to portray these moments. These can be recorded with a digital camera. Through shared writing the groups write accompanying text for their picture/image, either in full or as a caption.	Unit 2, drama activity 8
Instructions	Paired improvisation	In pairs, one child gives verbal instructions to the other who enacts exactly what is asked. The task to be instructed is agreed in advance and directly links to the drama. The instructions may then be listed and numbered.	Unit 1, drama activity 4
Lists	Working in role Occupational mime	Ask the children to list the jobs they need to do in role.	Unit 2, drama activity 2
Signs	Working in role Occupational mime	Make a stall sign for the Isle of Struay Show.	Unit 2, drama activity 3
Own version of story	Teacher-in-role Eye-witnesses	Following an incident in the drama ask children to relate what has just happened from their character's viewpoint, e.g. as an eye-witness talking to a blind man. You could give opportunity for the class to listen to different characters telling the scene in turn, before they write their version of events.	Unit 4, drama activity 12

Text type	Supporting drama strategy	Drama activity	Example unit / drama activity reference in Part 2
Character profiles Portraits Sketches	Role on the wall Hot-seating	Have outlines of a key character displayed and at key points in the drama invite the children to record what they know or feel about the character on self adhesive re-usable labels which they place around the outline. The characters can be interviewed first. These can be the basis for a character development study as the drama progresses.	Unit 3, drama activity 2
Questions	Hot-seating	Children decide on a question in advance that they will ask a character they are about to interview. Questions could be recorded and displayed on paper strips.	Unit 5, drama activity 14
Non-chronological reports	Mantle of the expert	Within a drama the children take on the role of 'experts' in some field, and are required to produce an in-role report or log, which can be written, e.g. information on wolves in response to the King's request. Research may be required, possibly using the Internet.	Unit 4, drama activity 4 and 5
Poetic sentences Substitute own ideas as lines of poetry Use structure to write about own experience in similar form	Small group play-making Improvisation Still image	In groups, create additional scenes to those in the original poem, e.g. improvise new scenes about what else the Lady saw in her mirror and then write lines of linked poetry.	Unit 8, part 2, drama activity 1

Text type	Supporting drama strategy	Drama activity	Example unit / drama activity reference in Part 2
Ordering events Story structure Story plan Sequence	Freeze-frame Tableau	Ask groups to list key moments in the story (possibly on strips of paper) and then freeze-frame one. Each group presents its freeze-frame in order.	Unit 7, drama activity 18
Written recounts of personal experience/ thought-bubbles/ diary/to record reflections	Improvisation Thought-tracking	Ask the children to recount and record their thoughts and feelings in role at a key point in the drama, possibly as preparation for writing in role.	Unit 8, part 3, drama activity 6
Write different story in same setting	Improvisation	Any drama involving improvisation based around an existing story will result in a different story, which can take place in the agreed same setting.	Unit 1, drama activity 6
Graffiti	Thought-tracking	Ask the children to imagine that graffiti about Macbeth starts to appear. Write it on an imaginary castle wall. Graffiti can be left on display and altered by different characters at different points in the story.	Unit 10, drama activity 5
Passages of dialogue Simple playscripts	Paired improvisation Small group play-making	After improvising in pairs the conversation can become recorded as written dialogue, which in turn could be playscripted.	Unit 5, drama activity 8
Settings descriptions Re-describe story settings	Ritual	Ask the children in turn to describe the imaginary setting in role as if they are there. Each child starts with the same opening phrase, 'I can see . . .' or 'I can hear . . .'	Unit 8, part 1, drama activity 4 Unit 6, drama activity 1

Text type	Supporting drama strategy	Drama activity	Example unit / drama activity reference in Part 2
Notes Jottings	Communal voice Hot-seating	Interview characters and take notes as a record.	Unit 6, drama activity 5
Storyboards Captions Thought bubbles Speech bubbles	Freeze-frame Tableau improvis-ation Thought-tracking Performance carousel	A series of freeze-frames can form the basis of a sequenced living storyboard or photograph album, with the children creating the images. Digital photographs can be used to record the images. Speech or thoughts for each character can be enacted and then added to the digital image in thought bubbles and captions.	Unit 3, drama activity 3
Letters Persuasive writing	Decision alley	Letters to inform or influence absent characters in the drama can be written, e.g. a letter to Theseus from a royal adviser.	Unit 7, drama activity 7
Rules	Improvisation	Drama that involves communities can be strengthened by agreeing, recording and displaying community rules, e.g. Park rules.	Unit 2, drama activity 7
Messages	Improvisation Teacher-in-role	The teacher can act as an intermediary offering to take messages to characters who are absent from the scene. These messages can be written with the childrens' guidance whilst the teacher scribes.	Unit 6, drama activity 6

Text type	Supporting drama strategy	Drama activity	Example unit / drama activity reference in Part 2
Headlines Newspaper reports	Freeze-frame Hot-seating	Newsworthy still images can be turned into newspaper photographs, with the children writing accompanying reports. Characters can be interviewed by reporters. Headlines can be added. Conversely a headline can be the stimulus for creating a group still image which then is brought to life through improvisation.	Unit 2, drama activity 8
News report Verbal report as journalist on imagined events	Freeze-frame Hot-seating	As above but the item is prepared as a radio or TV news report.	Unit 10, drama activity 8
Explanations of process	Mantle of the expert	Within the drama 'experts' may have reason to explain a process to someone (e.g. jam tart making to the Queen of Hearts).	Unit 1, drama activity 4
'For' and 'against' columns Character's dilemma Present a point of view Construct effective arguments Balanced report	Decision alley Collective voice	At moments of indecision for a character, two lines of children speak aloud the opposing voices in the character's mind. The thoughts can be listed in two columns and form the basis of persuasive writing from two viewpoints (e.g. should the hungry boy in the forest be fed?).	Unit 6, drama activity 8
Advertisement	Improvisation	Problems within a drama story can lead to the need to recruit someone through an advertisement, for example for a suitable prospective wife for the King.	Unit 6, drama activity 5

Text type	Supporting drama strategy	Drama activity	Example unit / drama activity reference in Part 2
Recount same event in a variety of ways/ write from another Character's viewpoint Story notes for Storytelling Manipulating narrative	Storytelling	Ask the children at the end of a drama to list key events, using a minimum number of sentences. These become storytelling prompts for different characters to retell the story from the viewpoint.	Unit 3, drama activity 14, Unit 7, drama activity 17
Journal	Reflection in role Thought-tracking	At different key points in the drama the children can write a journal section in role as a reflective record of their viewpoint as a character (e.g. Lady Macbeth's diary).	Unit 10, drama activity 7
Petition	Teacher-in-role Improvisation	Reasons for protest within a drama can result in a reason in role to create a petition (e.g. villagers petitioning the King about the need to capture the wolf).	Unit 4, drama activity 2
Describe person from different perspectives	Hot-seating Thought-tracking	Hot-seat different characters who know a particular character in order to get their perspective (e.g. views of different Athenians about Theseus going to slay the Minotaur).	Unit 7, drama activity 9
Flashbacks	Freeze-frame	Ask the children to make a still image to represent a past moment in the drama. This can be given a narrated past tense narrative (e.g. the moment Macbeth stabs Duncan).	Unit 10, drama activity 6

Text type	Supporting drama strategy	Drama activity	Example unit / drama activity reference in Part 2
Alternative endings Write new scenes Annotate playscript section	Small group play-making Forum theatre	Ask different groups to replay the end scene of a drama to show alternative endings which can then be written up as prose or playscript.	Unit 10, drama activity 8
Questionnaires	Hot-seating	Before interviewing a character the children can be asked to list individually or together the questions they want to ask. Teachers can restrict the number of questions.	Unit 5, drama activity 14
Legal documents	Teacher-in-role	Reasons sometimes arise for a pretend legal document within a drama (e.g. proof of sale or a formal contract between two parties).	Unit 5, drama activity 13

Drama and Thinking Skills

4

> *When I examine myself and my methods of thought, I come to the conclusion that the gift of fantasy has meant more to me than my talent for absorbing positive knowledge.*
>
> (Einstein)

The National Curriculum stresses the importance of children developing thinking skills, 'knowing how' and not just 'knowing what'. Drama in education is a process, just as thinking is a process and at its core is the engagement of children's thinking. Drama in education can be based on anything subject-wise but it is the socially mediated process of emotionally engaging, exploring, devising, expressing, communicating and making meaning together, in short, thinking, that is central to it.

High quality drama shares many characteristics with the criteria of high quality thinking (Table 4.1). Indeed the criteria which Resnick defined, are almost synonymous with drama.

The development of children's thinking involves the development of perception and sensory awareness as well as cognitive skills. Young children take in the world primarily and initially through their senses and analyse their sensory experiences through thought. They need to actively engage with experience in order to learn, and this has long been recognised.

> *I hear, I know. I see, I remember. I do, I understand.*
>
> (Confucius 551 BC–479 BC)

In drama, we are inviting children to bring their memories and previous learning and real-life experiences to an active, creative fictitious experience with fellow participants, to think in and out of role and thus to engage and empathise with a range of issues and situations from different perspectives.

Children bring from the real world to the drama, what they already know, consciously and sub-consciously and the teacher's task is to offer structure and strategies to help children to move their thinking forward, to imagine, recognise, stay in and develop their thinking within and about key moments, to explore and reflect on these moments socially, physically, cognitively, emotionally, spiritually, morally and culturally.

Table 4.1 Linking high quality thinking processes and the drama process

High quality thinking	High quality drama
Is not routine – the path of action is not fully known in advance	Is not just re-enactment of what is known. The children make decisions that influence the direction of the drama and they are given ownership, with their ideas being used to develop the drama.
Tends to be complex – the total path is not visible from a single viewpoint	Drama explores through role the same situation from the viewpoints of different characters. It is not a linear process.
Yields multiple rather than unique solutions	Drama is 'open'. Scenes can be reworked and replayed in many ways with a multiplicity of solutions and outcomes.
Involves nuanced judgement and interpretation	Nuance is key to drama. Meanings are arrived at and communicated in a variety of ways, verbal, visual and kinaesthetic. Each person in an audience and each participant in the drama will interpret the drama somewhat differently, depending on their present understandings and experience.
Can involve the application of multiple criteria, which may conflict with one another	Drama involves problem-solving and the resolution of dilemmas both within the drama and in the process of making the drama.
Involves uncertainty – not everything about the task at hand is known	Drama in education develops. It cannot be known what will emerge in the process as it is interactive and dynamic by nature. It is not about re-enacting what is known and certain, but about discovering and exploring what is uncertain.
Involves imposing meaning – finding structure in apparent disorder	Drama is all about finding, making and communicating meanings. It is structured, mainly by the teacher initially, but as children become more experienced and develop their drama skills they are more able to take over responsibility for structuring their own drama and communicating meaning to others through performance.
Is effortful – considerable mental work is needed for the kinds of elaboration and judgements required	Good drama is an active and interactive experience, which is both intellectually and emotionally demanding for both participants and audience.

Adapted from HMSO (1999)

Within the drama experience, children are required to actively imagine and to process information through the use of language and other symbolic forms. Drama gives opportunity for both freedom and discipline of thought simultaneously. Children are given the freedom to develop their own ideas and create together within the conventions and structures that drama as an art form provides.

Within the drama the children actively generate ideas that are original to them and regenerate and experiment with previous ideas in new fictitious social contexts. They think through situations in role and act upon their ideas in a safe supportive forum. Their thinking is valued and accepted by the teacher and the group. It guides the development and direction of the drama itself.

With the teacher working alongside them in a parallel role, they have the benefit of a model who ostensibly is thinking alongside them, grappling with the same issues, dilemmas, challenges and moments of indecision within the drama. The teacher is able to intervene, question and challenge from within the fiction, to think out loud alongside the children, to model thinking physically, verbally and symbolically. The teacher in role can provide an immediate or timed response to the children's thoughts and actions and can coach their thinking, deciding when to fade, withdraw or intervene. The teacher is alongside the children at the time that they are cognitive processing. Later, out of drama mode, the teacher is able to support the transfer of learning by explicitly highlighting and making conscious the links with other areas of learning (e.g. children may participate in a drama which resolves an issue relating to bullying without then necessarily transferring what they have thought, felt and articulated into their everyday lives). The drama can provide in the future a shared reference point with which they have all hopefully emotionally engaged and reflected upon.

Three combined processes determine success in thinking:

- input – obtaining and organising knowledge through sensory awareness and perception to confirm 'what I know';
- control – thinking through a situation and making actions meaningful, for example, planning, decision-making and evaluating;
- output – strategies for using knowledge and solving problems that combine 'what I do' with 'what I know', for example, remembering and thinking about and generating new ideas.

(QCA 2001)

Through using well-focused drama strategies, the teacher enables children to organise knowledge in ways that use and develop sensory awareness. They use vision, hearing and touch. Drama provides contexts which motivate the children to think and within which actions and objects take on meaning. Objects, events and experiences are linked as the children develop their understanding of symbolism and symbolic form. The children are given or create their own engaging imaginary situations and issues to explore actively together. They are empowered to play and experiment with their thoughts and ideas within the drama forum. Protected by working in role, they are asked to remember, to generate and explore ideas, to predict and anticipate, to solve imaginary problems together, to make decisions and act on them, to consider the consequences of their actions and decisions on others. Through carefully structured drama children can be given the opportunity to exercise and develop a wide range of thinking skills (Figure 4.1).

	Teacher comments
Sequencing and ordering information	
Sorting, classifying, grouping, analysing	
Identifying part/whole relationships	
Comparing and contrasting	
Making predictions and hypothesising	
Drawing conclusions	
Giving reasons for conclusions	
Distinguishing fact from opinion	
Determining bias and checking the reliability of evidence	
Generating new ideas and brainstorming	
Relating cause and effect	
Devising a fair test	
Defining and clarifying problems	
Thinking up different solutions	
Setting up goals and sub-goals	
Testing solutions and evaluating outcomes	
Planning and monitoring progress towards a goal	
Revising plans	
Making decisions	
Setting priorities	
Weighing up pros and cons	

Figure 4.1. Record/checklist of different kinds of thinking skills (after Swartz and Parks 1994). Adapted from HMSO (1999).

The drama builds individual and collective meanings, which the children are then supported to reflect on both in and out of role. Reflection is crucial to the development of successful thinking and drama builds in reflective opportunities during and at the end of the lesson. Although the children are thinking and working in role, they are ever present in the experience as themselves, and after thinking as a character in an imagined world, these thoughts remain with them as they carry them back into the real world. The drama provides an exciting and safe forum for thinking and acting behind the shield of a role, but once the shield is removed, the experience and thoughts from the drama remain with the child cognitively and maybe emotionally.

> *Thinking takes place in a social context and is influenced by the culture and environment in which the children learn.* (QCA 2001)

Drama is a social and cultural activity. The children bring their own cultural understanding to it and further develop their cultural understanding through it. Indeed, through the creation of performance for others they may themselves contribute to our constantly developing culture.

5 Drama and Information and Communications Technology (ICT)

There has been an escalation of computer literacy among children during the last decade, mainly as a result of increased access to home computers. Computer technology is now part of children's culture and will continue to penetrate, broaden and disturb the popular meaning of literacy. Many children are coming into school with sophisticated computer skills which have been developed from an early age. In turn, teachers have had to rapidly develop their own computer skills in order to provide a challenging, integrated ICT curriculum. ICT is now a learning tool across the curriculum, including the drama curriculum, and is not just a bolt-on subject.

We live in a society dominated by the written word and need to move towards a different understanding more in line with children's culture. The future could present to educators a situation where computer illiteracy might carry the same stigma as being illiterate. The integration of ICT into the curriculum therefore is not only an essential strand in a well-balanced and broad curriculum but every child's educational entitlement.

The NLS suggests that children need to:
• compare the way information is presented, to use IT to bring work to a published form; • to investigate how reading strategies are adapted to suit the different properties of IT texts.

However, apart from this, the use of ICT within drama has powerful connotations. The dynamic nature of the art form is transitory and dependent on the fusion between reality and imagination. Through technology this can become permanent and substantial. Moments can be captured, sequences manipulated, subtexts revealed and metaphors reflected by the sheer immediacy and potential to manipulate which ICT presents. It is this, and willingness to embrace change in the nature of the art form, which can incorporate ICT into teaching and learning and support the making and communicating of meaning, as central to drama in the learning process.

Computers can be used within the context of the drama itself. For example, emailing an absent character and awaiting their reply, which could be devised and sent later, possibly by the teacher. This allows the convincing creation of a character who can influence the drama without being physically present, a sort of absent 'teacher in role'.

The use of a digital camera within the drama is a different convention based in a visual mode of communication. Media, like drama, connects visual image and story. Popular culture, especially through television and film, has provided children with a rich experience in visual sound communication and this, through the digital camera, can work together with conventional drama strategies and widen their potential. Indeed, terminology used in drama may be shared with media terminology, for example 'freeze-frame' is media linked. Also, teachers who are aware of children's media literacy may use media language to help the children understand the drama and its structures, e.g. 'Let's fast-forward and see what happens.' Teachers may liken drama to video for children by explaining that drama, like video, can hold moments still (still image/freeze-frame, tableau, storyboard), go forwards (improvisation and play-making) or backwards (re-wind to past freeze-frames). We can turn down the sound and have action only (mime) or hear the soundtrack without a visual image (sound-collage or soundtrack). We can select out and edit, replay scenes and moments, dubbing different speech (improvisation) and thoughts (thought-tracking). We can, with the advent of digital television, interact with the screen (forum-theatre) and change the storyline by selecting different multi-paths (play-making and alternative scripts).

A digital camera takes single and multi-shot pictures, records five- or six-second sound-bytes and can be shown on screen, allowing a scene to be read immediately it is finished. It provides both teacher and learner with valuable opportunities. It allows children to be both participants and their own audience, to see themselves, discuss and evaluate their own performances and those of peers, and develop their ideas and skills. It creates a situation where both participants and audience can read images together and revisit them. Crucial moments in the drama can be recorded to enable children to focus on meaning in both abstract and concrete forms. Downloading images from a digital camera onto a screen gives the children the freedom to manipulate sequences, change chronological order, predict, reveal subtext and create alternative characters and stories. A digital camera within the drama can become one of the characters, a 'fly on the wall' or indeed 'look' with any kind of eye – sympathetic, critical, cruel, condoning – so adding a fascinating additional creative dimension to the children's work.

Software such as PowerPoint or Mediator can be used as a means of recording findings, presenting a range of drama activities combined with graphics and techniques available in these programmes. Digital images can be made of the children's freeze-frame work from a text and made into a picture book or storyboard of the alternative story, possibly with thought or speech bubbles with text and captions added.

The Internet can also be a powerful source of information and images that can support or develop dramas. For example, if children need to take on the role of wolf experts who have been summoned to appear before the King, then they may be motivated to carry out an Internet search for 'wolf facts' first in order to convincingly adopt 'the mantle of the expert'. The King may inform them in advance of the questions he will require his wolf experts to answer.

Assessment in and through Drama

6

Assessment has always been deemed difficult in the arts. How can one assess something that is so inherently subjective? Drama, however, is not only a learning medium but an art form, with its own distinctive theatrical skills, knowledge, skills and understanding. This wealth of knowledge, culture and tradition is at the disposal of every teacher to use, to enrich their teaching and enhance the potency of children's learning.

Assessment is as central to drama as it is to any other area of the curriculum, because drama, whether it is within English or as an arts subject, is part of the learning process and significant in the drive to raise standards. Assessment promotes and records effective learning and informs planning. It is, therefore, an essential tool in both teaching and learning. In drama the teacher, as observer and participant, can often open up significant areas for assessment, which can remain difficult to access through more traditional teaching.

Difficulties in assessment in the arts can be associated with the division between formative and summative forms, between the assessment of process and that of product. There is, however, an interrelationship between the two, with one feeding into the other, i.e. assessment during the learning process informs the next steps in relation to what needs to be learned. Measurement and precise, efficient, testing are not well suited to many aspects of learning in the arts and it is vital that arts subjects and forms are assessed in appropriate ways. Inappropriate existing assessment models must not be forced to fit. Teachers need to assess what they value both in drama and when using drama skills and approaches in other curriculum areas, including literacy. Drama lends itself readily to the analysis of process as well as product. However, in drama, process and product are inseparable and can indicate the levels of children's development across a range of areas.

Formative assessment that informs and promotes learning is embedded in the developing drama. Through in-role observation and participation and through out-of-role observation the teacher can move in close during the process or distance themselves as assessors of the product. Through appropriate intervention and interaction in and out of role, the teacher can pose questions, provide opportunities that generate ideas which move the fiction on, and focus on significant moments and events which reveal the depth of the children's understanding and commitment. Through observation and participation within the drama the teacher can assess the children's ability to assume and sustain a role and to communicate ideas both individually and collectively though drama form.

Assessment to inform and develop learning should involve sharing criteria first, in order to help children to recognise standards and expectations and to evaluate their own success. When children know what the teacher is looking for in an effective, successful, still image, for example, they will be more able to create one and then judge whether they (and their peers) have succeeded. Self-assessment and peer assessment can enrich teacher assessment and encourage children to recognise and chart their own progress and improvement as long as children are informed of the criteria.

Assessing both process and product can be looked at in three interrelated areas:
• cognitive and affective understanding • understanding and development of drama skills and forms • personal and social development

Assessment of children's learning and progress in drama

There are many models that have been used to assess drama but there is no generally accepted model in common use in primary education. A helpful proforma for assessing the strands of speaking and listening (including drama) is contained in *Teaching Speaking and Listening in Key Stages 1 and 2*, pages 14 and 15 (QCA 1999). The following model is a further development and adaptation of this, which offers more detailed criteria for the assessment of the drama strand.

It is intended that teachers select assessment questions appropriate to the task from the drama-specific areas of cognitive and affective understanding, and drama skills and forms. The more implicit areas of personal and social development can be reflected on in conjunction with other areas of the curriculum, and the overall pattern of progress and modes of behaviour (Figure 6.1).

Through this assessment procedure teachers can:
• record significant verbal contributions of children which provide evidence to support levelling in speaking and listening; • assess speaking and listening, reading and writing through a range of tasks generated by and within the drama; • record an evidence base generated by the drama work for external purposes; • inform future planning.

Drama record sheet

Name:	National Curriculum Year: Term:

Cognitive and affective capabilities:	Activity/date	Assessment comments
To work imaginatively to improvise and sustain a role		
Through action and language create in a make-believe context		
To use drama to approach writing in and out of role		
To make constructive contributions to imagined problem-solving and decision-making		
To differentiate between character		
To invent imagined settings, characters and plots, adapt and extend ideas, to empathise with and speculate about characters		

Figure 6.1 Drama record sheet.

Personal and social capabilities:	**Activity/date**	**Assessment comments**
To collaborate and reach agreement		
To interact and negotiate verbally with others		
To engage emotionally through drama activities with text		
To explore meaning individually and collectively		
To work with others in performance		
Gain confidence and develop their own and others self-esteem		

Understanding and development of drama skills and forms. Capabilities:	**Activity/date**	**Assessment comments**
To use drama skills and forms to communicate ideas		
To recognise elements of theatre and how this can create performance		
To devise and evaluate plays		
To realise the need to use voice and movement in different ways to express emotion, describe situations and portray character		
To accept and identify different cultural language features and conventions		
To understand the relationship between audience and participant		
Next steps:		

Areas for assessment

Questions to reflect on – can the children:
• work imaginatively in a make-believe context; • invent imagined settings, characters and situations; • engage in and identify with drama activities using appropriate language and actions; • extend ideas within the drama; • reflect on meaning explored within the drama; • interact and collaborate with others and exchange and develop ideas generously and sensitively; • collectively explore meaning and form creatively; • respect each others contributions and accept challenges; • draw on drama skills to communicate their ideas; • understand elements of theatre.

Assessment tasks

To provide:
• set assessment tasks (e.g. writing and drawing) which will inform the drama and provide evidence of learning; • opportunities for children to self-assess formatively.
Record, assess and collect:
• the significant verbal contributions of children, which provide evidence to support levelling in speaking and listening; • speaking and listening, reading and writing through tasks generated by and within the drama; • an evidence base generated by the drama work to share with parents and others as evidence of learning and progression.

7 Drama Strategies and Conventions

Introduction

Powerful and meaningful drama has to be structured and planned whilst enabling freedom and space within its structure for the children to think and create for themselves. Strategies or conventions are instrumental in providing a safe and understood framework for both teacher and learner. When children and teachers become increasingly familiar with strategies, activities and conventions, they can play with them, explore the strategies, experiment with them, adapt and refine them, to make them their own vehicles for the exploration, making and communication of meaning.

Strategies can be adapted to meet specific needs and learning objectives. They can be extended or restricted, invented, repeated and discarded. The concept of strategies is flexible and part of the dramatic and changing nature of the art form. Experienced drama teachers know what will engage the children's interest, and what they want the children to learn. They can structure their lessons to provide opportunities to explore issues and empathise with the experience of others.

Teachers can select and adapt strategies to develop skills and consider other viewpoints. They structure the drama in a way that engages the children and are sensitive to the way the lesson is developing. They decide when to listen and observe, when to act or interact in or out of role and when to intervene or stop the drama. They use the children's own ideas and contributions, when possible, to feed into and develop the drama. They decide how they can most profitably be involved in the drama to support the children's learning. Sometimes the teacher will facilitate and at other times direct. The teacher makes whatever moves are necessary, selects whatever is the most appropriate strategy, to keep the drama developing, to keep the children involved, thinking and learning.

The teacher will have clearly defined the learning objectives but the route to achieving those objectives can be open to negotiation as the drama unfolds through the imaginations of the children and the teacher's framework of strategies. As children become increasingly conversant with the drama strategies, vocabulary and forms, they can be empowered to increasingly select strategies and forms for themselves that best communicate and express their meanings, thus becoming drama playwrights, producers and directors.

Improvisation

Improvisation is used frequently in drama activities. It is a means whereby participants in drama, by speaking and moving spontaneously, can create imaginary situations and actively explore human relationships, behaviour and events in role. It provides genuine contexts for speaking and listening, interaction and characterisation. The stimulus for improvisation can be from a text, a theme, an historical event, a social issue or simply an idea. Most spontaneous improvisation is not intended for presentation or repetition, however it is possible to isolate and replay or refine presentations of specific and significant events that were first devised through improvisation. These can be shared in order to move the drama forward, or focus more deeply on the issues, consequences and possible outcomes of an action or sequence.

Teacher-in-role

This is arguably the most powerful drama strategy and involves the teacher taking a role or a range of different roles. Although teachers can do drama lessons without being in role themselves, teacher-in-role signals that make-believe, imagination and creativity are valued and promoted by the teacher. It is highly engaging to children and does not require acting ability. It requires commitment and seriousness on the part of the teacher who has to present a set of attitudes, information or a viewpoint, rather than a great acting performance. Through this the teacher can support, develop and challenge the children's thinking from inside the drama as a fellow participant. Teachers should decide the function and purpose of their being in role and stay in role only as long as is necessary to achieve this.

The teacher may select a role that is dominant or high status, controlling the drama from within and making decisions. High status roles are often most comfortable for teachers new to drama and concerned about loss of control but high status roles are less often taken by experienced teachers as they can inhibit pupil response. The teacher can adopt a subordinate role, lower in order, rank and power, which implicitly raises the status of the children, empowering them to take control and develop their ideas within the drama. It can be useful for teachers to take a flexible intermediary or mid-status role, possibly to gather information or to disseminate information on behalf of a more powerful person or authority not present. The role of visitor, messenger or observer would serve this purpose and enable the teacher to decide whether to be a neutral intermediary or whether to take the children's side or not in relation to issues and events.

Teacher-in-role extends the possibilities and challenges the usual teacher and pupil status relationship, enabling teacher and learner to work in role together. It is advisable to discuss this strategy with the children first and to indicate clearly when the teacher is in or out of role. This can be done by positioning, by sitting down or standing up or the use of a prop or a piece of costume.

Freeze-frame, still image and tableau

This is a versatile strategy, which falls into two broad categories. Freeze-framing enables the teacher to stop the dramatic action, holding that moment still in time. It encourages deepening concentration and supports the critical analysis of key moments. It can also stop the drama moving at too fast a pace, disintegrating or becoming superficial. It can generate discussion around moments and encourage shared reflection and evaluation. It can provide a still visual image to which speech and thoughts can be added.

Still image has a variety of categories but, however it is named, sets out to create a still picture, photograph, sculpture or tableau. Attention needs to be given to the composition of the image and the most effective way to communicate the meaning embodied in the image. It can be representational or symbolic of an event, emotion or concept. Elements of theatre such as focus and tension need to be incorporated, as well as the way in which space and time can be an influence on the overall effect.

Still images can be put together to form sequences, posing theatrical problems to be solved, such as how the group (whether it be small or large) gets from one image to the next (see 'performance carousel', p. 51). Beginnings and endings need to be considered and the way in which the atmosphere of the image can best be communicated. Both these strategies could incorporate a narrator or caption to provide coherence and context.

'Mantle of the expert'

This involves children taking on roles that enable them to become experts within the drama. For example, as experts on wolves in 'The Last Wolf' they are required to produce an in-role report which can be both written and spoken, giving the King the information he needs. This will require research and planning as well as developing written and presentational skills. 'Mantle of the expert' raises children's levels of self-esteem and creates a sense of importance and worth. It facilitates children learning 'as if' as opposed to learning about.

Thought-tracking

The strategy of thought-tracking involves asking the children to share their 'in-role thoughts' by speaking them aloud. This can be done simply by stopping the drama and asking what each child is thinking or, alternatively, in a more theatrical and stylised way, with each child invited to speak their thoughts in role aloud as the teacher passes by them. This can be used to slow the drama down and encourage individual and shared reflection, particularly at key moments.

Thought-tracking can be used during or after freeze-frame or still image to draw out individual responses. The difference between speech and thought can be emphasised through this strategy: that what characters are saying is not necessarily what they are thinking. Through thought-tracking, subtexts and sub-plots can be revealed as spoken text, making visual and oral the multilayered and inferential aspects of the drama.

Teacher narrative

Narrative has a range of possible functions and purposes at different stages of the drama. It can start a session while children are carrying out occupational mime, thus assisting the building of a shared imaginary context, helping to establish the imaginary setting and shape the story.

Narrative storytelling is also an effective way of moving the drama on in time, retelling as story what the children have created so far, and introducing new information. It can change the pace and give form and shape to the activity. The narrative can be used to create atmosphere, build tension and focus on significant aspects of the drama. Through this the teacher, as storyteller, can provide a linguistic model for the children that may then be reflected in their own narrative speech and writing.

Like many of these strategies, narrative may also provide control within the context of the drama, and reflection as a way of bringing the children to a realisation or conclusion.

Hot-seating

This is a popular strategy, which is also versatile, but has the potential to be superficial. At its most shallow level the teacher or a child is placed in 'the hot seat' as a character from the drama and questioned openly about their feelings and motives in relation to themselves and the drama. At its best, it is a probing, demanding way of developing characterisation and refining the way in which children can begin to understand the complexity of questioning, and explore the sophisticated techniques of asking questions in order to unearth information. The success of this strategy comes from the children's awareness that both the person in the 'hot seat' and the questioners are of equal importance to the drama. Children need time to consider their questions, what they want to know about the character in the 'hot seat' and to formulate their questions to extract this information.

Decision alley

Decision alley can be used when a character is required to consider a course of action and make a decision. It needs to be used when there are different choices to be made, conflicting interests and dilemmas to be resolved. The children, in role as other characters with viewpoints to share, make 'the alley' by forming two lines facing each other. The character who has to make the decision walks slowly between the two lines listening to the warnings and persuasive advice offered by the other characters. At the end of the line a decision has to be made. The lines may represent contrasting viewpoints, or they may be random, however it is important that the character's conflict is resolved by the end. The fact that the character is undecided and can be influenced by the children's powers of persuasion is motivating. Usually each child is invited to speak to the indecisive character only once as they pass by. The conflicting thoughts and voices in the character's head can be likened to the character's conscience speaking to him at a key moment.

Ritual

Ritual as an important element of theatre and the culture of our daily lives can fulfil similar roles in teaching. It can be used to focus attention and to mark significant moments in the drama. Once established, rituals can be used repeatedly and provide a secure reference point for participation and a sense of community. Different forms of spoken language and stylised action can be used to support the formality of the ritual, possibly devised by the teacher using the children's suggestions for younger children. Older children might devise their own rituals, developing their understanding of cultural symbolism.

Telephone conversations

The use of telephones is a primary means of communication for children. The acceptance too of the mobile phone has added another interesting dimension to this strategy in drama. Telephone conversations can involve children in pairs holding imaginary conversations at a particular point in the drama, and individuals speaking on telephones and inferring the other conversation. However, mobile phone conversations can be used at any time in the drama plot, in any setting, by any character to impart and receive information, to build tension, to create and solve problems. They can be used to consolidate or destroy relationships, to introduce new characters and move the drama forward. They may be overheard or participated in.

Role on the wall

This strategy can make visual a particular character important in the development of the drama. The character is represented by a picture, a photograph or a life-size outline which is displayed in a prominent position. This serves as a focal point for deepening the understanding of the character. Children contribute by speaking or writing their ideas and thoughts on the image; information and feelings for the character can be written, the viewpoints of other characters noted, and consideration given to the thoughts and opinions of the central character. This can encourage empathy and deepen understanding of human behaviour. It may be helpful to sub-section the space around the character into three areas, headed 'What we know', 'What we think we know' and 'What we want to know' for each character. Suggestions can be written on self-adhesive removable labels. The role on the wall can be revisited at different points in the drama and labels removed or added as the character develops.

Forum theatre

This is an excellent way to develop the relationship between audience and participant and the idea of sharing ideas and critical reflective observation of drama. A group of children improvise a significant part of the drama to the rest of the class who have an opportunity to comment on the action and make suggestions to develop the work. The audience can stop the drama, suggest changes in positioning, focus and the interrelationship of characters. If appropriate they can remove, replace or introduce new characters to find the most effective way in which the drama can be performed. The audience can ask characters to replay scenes differently in order to study the differing outcomes. Through this strategy children are not only exploring situations created by the drama, but also developing their skills and understanding of the art form as producers and directors.

Mime and movement

The use of mime and movement as a chosen strategy enables children to work kinaesthetically and concentrate on gesture, facial expression, body language and movement. It is valuable in creating an imaginary context or character, and for some children changes the immediate pressure to speak. It can be used in conjunction with thought-tracking or freeze-frame and provide an opportunity for the children to experiment with fragmented language and voice collage, which can dramatically enhance their drama sequences. Soundtracking or sound-collage can be used very successfully to accompany mime and movement to build atmosphere and establish environments. Children can experiment with voice, body or percussion sounds in an expressive and creative way.

Choral speaking

Choral speaking has theatrical roots and has played a particular role in the development of the theatre. As a teaching strategy it has potential in both the interpretation and performance of poetry and as an exciting and creative way to develop narration. Individual voices can be used to establish character or to focus on statements, questions or thoughts. Lines can be spoken in unison, overlay each other or be spoken as a round. Volume, speed, pause and rhythm can all contribute to the dramatic effect of choral speech.

Speaking objects

This involves each child positioning themselves as an object within a scene (e.g. the Lady of Shalott's hairbrush). The objects can in turn speak about themselves in relation to a character or event, as eye-witness with a viewpoint. They can speak freely at a given signal or answer questions.

Active storytelling

Active storytelling at its simplest is a term used to describe children enacting a story as it is being told. It is from this that interactive storytelling emerges through the medium of drama.

Group play-making

Group play-making involves a group of children devising a scene for performance, usually to the rest of the class. It may develop from group improvisation but the children will then reshape it for an audience

Communal voice

This involves a group of children, possibly the whole class, taking on the role of one character together. They speak in turn following on in the linguistic style of the previous speaker and building on what has already been said. Done well, the collective effect is that we believe we have been listening to the voice of one person.

Drama games

The game can play an important role in drama, especially as a starting point or with children who have limited experience. It is important, however, to make sure that the game is in context, is appropriate to the content of the lesson and reflects the learning objectives such as the Rumour Game in 'The Lady of Shalott' (See Unit 8). Inappropriate, out-of-context games simply used as 'warm-up' activities can be counterproductive and make it difficult for the teacher to progress.

Guided visualisation

This strategy creates an opportunity for children to use their imaginative thinking to recall past experiences or begin to create new settings or situations.

This is an excellent way to start a new drama. By closing their eyes the children can concentrate on their sense of hearing in combination with their imagination. The teacher can read a description of a place using words to paint a picture 'in the mind's eye'. Children in groups can do this for each other by writing their own descriptions of landscapes and settings and reading these aloud to the rest of the class.

Performance carousel

This strategy provides an opportunity for groups to perform scenes individually and collectively, but within a collective context. Each group can prepare a scene representing a part of the drama story. They then arrange these in chronological order and perform them in sequence without interruption, either on a signal from the teacher or from a cue or understanding devised by each group. Before and after performance, groups need to freeze. This merges the idea of audience and participant, and encourages interdependence and a theatrical awareness of drama as an art form.

Essence machine (or theatre machine)

Essence machine is movement- and sound-based. It is designed to give children the opportunity to work in a more abstract, synthesised and stylistic way, to create an evocative landscape which can provide the multi-sensory environment for narration, dramatic action and dialogue

Eavesdropping

Overheard conversations, which can be reported at a later stage in the drama, allow the children to move the action on and can have the potential to influence and broaden the storyline.

Eye-witness

Eye-witness provides a strategy which enables the children to recall a part of the drama and report back from their own character's viewpoint.

Working in role

This strategy gives children the opportunity to take on the role of another character. Working 'as if' as opposed to learning about. This structured role-play enables children to empathise with others and experience different modes of behaviour within the context of the drama.

Part 2

Practical Units

Introduction

Units

Each unit is planned for different year groups and is intended to provide continuity and progression. Some units span two vertical year groups. Teachers may feel able to adapt units for different ages, although the type of literature the unit is based on directly links to the literacy ranges given in the National Literacy Strategy Framework for Teaching for specific year groups.

Units linked to SATs reading comprehension

Unit 4 'The Last Wolf' and Unit 9 'The Asrai' are based on reading texts which have been used for the SATs reading comprehension tests at Key Stage 1 and Key Stage 2 respectively. The literacy and drama activities are designed to support children in answering linked SATs questions afterwards.

Range

Each unit is based on a different text. Where texts are named but not printed within the unit, an outline of the story has been given to enable teachers to use the unit without the text if desired. However, it is strongly recommended that children are given access to the full original text wherever possible.

Learning objectives

A list of possible learning objectives that can be met through the activities is given in each unit. The lists are not definitive and teachers may select certain key objectives as a focus or add others of their own. The objectives are taken directly from the NLS, sometimes with adaptation. Objectives are also taken and adapted from *Teaching Speaking and Listening in Key Stages 1 and 2*. Additional drama objectives have been included if appropriate.

Introductory literacy activities

All units are text-based and each unit commences with literacy based activities which are designed to directly engage and familiarise children with the text before moving them into further active exploration of the text through drama activities.

Possible drama activities

The drama activities are designed to enable the teacher to support the children in accessing the text and subtext actively through a range of multi-sensory activities that require them to use multi-intelligences. The drama activities are balanced to ensure that children are able to respond to the text verbally, visually and kinaesthetically.

Drama strategies

The drama activities are based on established and developed drama strategies which are named at the start of each activity. To understand more about how different strategies work and how to introduce and use them, teachers may refer to Chapter 7 in Part 1 of this book.

Writing opportunities

As the drama activities are developed they may provide engaging reasons for writing within the imagined context. Some opportunities have been highlighted. Again, these link directly with types of writing from the NLS framework.

Other integrated curricular opportunities

A limited but specific reference is made to other integrated curriculum opportunities such as those provided for the use and development of ICT.

Possible assessment focus

Some areas for assessment are highlighted at the end of each unit. Teachers may use these or prefer to focus on linked assessment areas of their own. The assessment foci are linked directly with the model presented in Part 1 of this book, which is an extension and development of the model offered in *Teaching Speaking and Listening at Key Stages 1 and 2*.

Unit 1 *The Queen of Hearts*

Foundation Stage: Reception year

Range

Fiction and poetry: nursery rhymes

The Queen of Hearts,
she made some tarts,
all on a summer day.
The Knave of Hearts
he stole those tarts
and took them clean away.

The King of Hearts
called for the tarts
and beat the Knave full sore.
The Knave of Hearts
brought back the tarts
and vowed he'd steal no more.

Learning objectives

- to respond to teacher-in-role to explore familiar nursery rhyme characters
- to respond in role to develop a story
- to practise the verbal sequencing of instructions
- to practise positional vocabulary kinaesthetically
- to approach shared writing in role for an imagined purpose
- to consider forgiveness and/or punishment

Introductory literacy activity

Introduce the nursery rhyme to the children by reading it or telling it to them. You may wish to draw the children's attention to the rhyming words and also ensure that they understand the storyline and who the main characters are.

Possible drama activities

1 Enactment

Retell the story through action, using conventional playing cards as characters (King, Queen, Jack of Hearts).

2 Working in role

Explain to the children that they can pretend to be in the story. They will be people who work in the royal kitchens. They have all received an invitation to the Grand Royal Summer Picnic (Literacy Support Sheet 1).

Writing opportunity

Reply to the invitation either using the reply slip (Literacy Support Sheet 1) or as an individual or a class letter.

3 Occupational mime

Ask the children to suggest appropriate tasks (depending on the space available) that they might be doing on the morning of the picnic (e.g. polishing cutlery, folding napkins, making sandwiches, etc.). Carry out the tasks individually or in pairs.

Shared writing opportunity

With teacher as scribe, create a list of tasks that need to be done.

4 Teacher-in-role/mantle of the expert

Establish with the children that when you are holding the playing card of the Queen of Hearts, you will be pretending to be her. Ensure that they understand when you are in or out of role. In role, tell the children that the King is requesting that the Queen personally make him jam tarts for the picnic. You are unable to make tarts without their guidance. Pretend that you cannot remember the recipe and are muddled. Ask them to give you verbal tart-making instructions. Afterwards leave the tarts cooking.

Shared writing opportunity

You could write a large copy of the instructions they dictate in sequence before miming them.

5 Ritual

Preferably seated in a class circle, discuss with the children their favourite picnic foods. In turn, each child has the opportunity to place an item of imaginary picnic food in the royal picnic basket. As they place their item, they complete the following sentence in turn 'I am going to the picnic and I am bringing . . .'

6 Teacher in role/mime/oral storytelling

Let the children become eye-witnesses as you mime locking the jam tarts inside the royal kitchen. Explain that this is necessary because the Knave of Hearts loves jam tarts and is not to be trusted.

Writing opportunity

Do the children have any stories to tell you about the naughty Knave? These could be written up or illustrated later in a class 'Naughty Knave Storybook'.

7 Mime (follow-my-leader)/teacher-in-role

This activity can be done on the spot if necessary. As the Queen, tell the children that the tarts have gone missing and the Knave is missing. Can they come with you to help find the Knave and recover the tarts? Perform a follow-my-leader journey and use this as an opportunity to introduce and reinforce positional vocabulary (e.g. through the gate, down the path, across the lawn, around the lake, etc.). Selected children could take turns to lead.

Writing/drawing opportunity

This activity could form the basis of a class-shared imaginary labelled route map.

8 Teacher-in-role/hot-seating/mantle of the expert

Holding the Knave/Jack of Hearts card, explain that you will now pretend to be the Knave. Confide in the children that you took the tarts but have not eaten any. You regret taking them and would like to return them but are too frightened. The King can get very angry. Can the children suggest a course of action for the Knave? Listen to and support the children's suggestions. Tell the children eventually that you have decided to write to the King because you are too frightened to face him.

> *Writing opportunity*
>
> As the Knave, explain that you cannot write. Will they help you by writing on your behalf? The children can choose a series of scribes to record what you want to say.

9 Teacher-in-role

Hold the King card and explain that you will now pretend to be the King. You have received the Knave's letter and want the children to advise you on whether you should punish the Knave and, if so, how. The Knave has returned the tarts.

The children can use the cards to improvise and enact possible outcomes.

Possible assessment focus

- Were the children able to improvise and sustain the roles through action?
- Which children were able to interact verbally with others in role?
- Which children were able to contribute to the scribed writing-in-role activities?

Unit 2 *Katie Morag and the Two Grandmothers*

by Mairi Hedderwick

Key Stage 1

NC year group 1

Range

Fiction: stories with familiar settings

Outline

Katie Morag has two grandmothers, Grannie Island and Granma Mainland. They are quite different and do not get on with each other.

It is the time of the year for the Isle of Struay Show and Granma Mainland is visiting for a holiday. Katie Morag and Grannie Island meet the boat and take Granma Mainland back to the Post Office. Katie Morag watches her unpack all her shampoos and special creams. Grannie Island is not impressed by such vanity and goes off to find her prize-winning sheep Alecina to get her ready for the show. Katie Morag goes to help and eventually they find Alecina in the Boggy Loch covered with peaty stains and not up to show standard. Grannie Island despairs until Katie Morag remembers Granma Mainland's shampoos which make her hair shiny and white.

Grannie Island and Katie Morag rush Alecina back to the Post Office and using all Granma Mainland's special brushes and shampoos restore Alecina to prize-winning standards just in time for the show.

Alecina wins first prize for the best fleece, and Katie Morag and Grannie Island share a special secret about Granma Mainland's 'fancy ways'. The grandmothers get on much better after this day.

Learning objectives

- to locate key moments in a story
- to respond in a fictional setting to develop a story
- to problem solve co-operatively in role
- to write in role for imagined purposes
- to read a visual text (illustration)

Introductory literacy activities

- Introduce the story and read it to or with the children
- What variety of names do they use to refer to their grandmothers, e.g. Granny, Grandma?
- Ask the children which are the most important moments in the story and agree the sequence with them. Write and display the moments as headings and allocate each heading to groups of four or five children. Each group in turn tells their part of the story in order:
  - o Granma Mainland arrives on the island
  - o Granny Island meets Granma Mainland in Struay Lass
  - o Preparation for the show gets underway
  - o Alecina goes missing and is found
  - o Granny Island and Katie Morag get Alecina ready for the show
  - o Alecina wins first prize. Katie Morag and Granny Island share a secret

Possible drama activities

1 Freeze-frame

With a partner make a still image/picture from the family photograph album that shows the hostility between the two grandmothers. These could be photographed using a digital camera.

Writing opportunity

Ask the children to write a caption to go with their photo.

2 Working in role/occupational mime/improvisation

Look at the illustration (Literacy Support Sheet 2) of the Summer Show preparations. Ask the children what jobs people are doing in the picture (i.e. hammering in tent pegs, unpacking trophies, drying cups, etc.). What other jobs do the children think will need to be done that are not being shown in the picture?

> *Writing opportunity*
>
> Write and display a list of the jobs that will need to be done. This could be done as a group or class list. Look at Literacy Support Sheet 2 and write in what they imagine the people are thinking or saying.

3 Freeze-frame/improvisation

Ask the children to make a still picture of themselves carrying out one of the jobs and bring the scene to life at an agreed signal. Move amongst the children in role, interacting with them as a fellow villager.

> *Writing opportunity*
>
> There are notices, posters and signs within the book illustrations of the Show. Discuss what other notices, posters and labels they might see at the Show and ask them to write some.

4 Thought-tracking

Ask the children to get into a class circle around an imaginary bog. Tell them that Alecina is in the bog. Ask them to speak their thoughts in turn as they look at the trapped, filthy sheep.

5 Improvisation/teacher-in-role

With you in role as Grannie Island, ask the children for their suggestions as to how to get the sheep out. Enact any reasonable suggestions and after a while enable the children to succeed in releasing the sheep.

6 Improvisation/working in role

In pairs ask the children to wash, comb and dry the sheep's fleece. One child could hold the sheep as the other cleans it. Suggest that they might talk to the sheep to calm her.

7 Improvisation/ritual

Form a show arena inside a large class circle. Each child has the opportunity to proudly parade an imaginary sheep around the inside of the arena and say a few words about their sheep if they wish. As show judge, the teacher can ask the owners questions about their sheep.

Writing/ICT opportunity

With the children, devise a simple Sheep Show entry form. Entry rules and regulations could be devised and recorded. Each child could complete entry information on a simple database, possibly with support. Alternatively this could be done on photocopied forms first.

8 Freeze-frame/still image

Ask the children to get into groups of four or five and make a still picture of the presentation of the Silver Trophy. Tell them that this picture will be appearing in the local newspaper. The still images can be photographed using a digital camera.

Writing/ICT opportunity

Ask the children to make up captions for their group photographs, or a newspaper headline for the show newspaper report.

Writing opportunity

Granma Mainland sends a postcard to a friend on the mainland.

Possible assessment focus

- Which children make constructive contributions to the imagined problem-solving activity?
- Which children are best able to sustain a role verbally?
- Are those children who contribute less verbally nonetheless appearing to be fully engaged with the drama?

Unit 3 *Voices in the Park*

by Anthony Browne

Key Stage 1

NC year group 2

Range

Fiction: stories with familiar settings

Outline

Charles' mother takes Charles and their pedigree dog, Victoria, for a walk in the park. Victoria runs off with a mongrel, whilst Charles goes off unnoticed to the playground with Smudge, a working class girl. Smudge has come to the park with her unemployed father, whom Charles' mum looks down on. Charles' mum panics when she discovers Charles is missing. Charles is found and his angry mother walks home with him in silence. Smudge, on the other hand, chatters happily to her father all the way home. It emerges that Charles has picked a flower for Smudge, which she takes home with her.

Learning objectives

- to link a story theme with own experiences (e.g. going missing, falling out with parents, playing in the park)
- to list points
- to identify and compare differences between scenes
- to write character profiles, e.g. simple descriptions, using key words and phrases
- to develop oral versions of stories from text
- to read and respond imaginatively
- to ask relevant questions
- to adopt roles appropriately in small and large groups
- to improvise as a way of responding and interpreting

Introductory literacy activities

- The story is told from the viewpoints of four characters. Read the story straight through, possibly with four selected children reading the voices.
- Read the 'First Voice' to the children. Ask the children what they *know* (textual reference) about Charles' mother. Secondly, ask them what they *think they know* (textual inference), and lastly what they *want to know* (enquiry). Their ideas can be recorded in three headed columns (see Literacy Support Sheet 7).

Possible drama activities

1 Hot-seating/teacher-in-role

Explain that when you sit in a particular chair, you will pretend to be Charles' mother. They may ask you questions and you will answer in role. Remain as true to the text and character as you can. You can add details that develop the character in line with the text. Afterwards, you could ask the children to look at the text and identify what was text-based and what was not.

2 Hot-seating

Read the 'Third Voice' aloud (i.e. Charles), or invite a child to do so. Again the children should be given opportunity to speak with and question the character.

Writing opportunity/role on the wall

Around a big outline of Charles, gather and write the children's suggestions as to how they would describe his character. They could write words on post-its and place them around the outline.

3 Still image

Tell the children that you want them to imagine that Charles and his mother have a family photo album at home. Ask the children to get into pairs as Charles and his mother and make themselves into a photograph from that album. They should decide where the photo was taken (e.g. first day at school, holiday, birthday, Christmas Day, etc.).

ICT/writing opportunity

The images could be recorded with a digital camera and thoughts in the form of captions added.

4 Thought-tracking/still image

Ask the children to hold their images as still as a photograph. Tell them that you will pass close by each image in turn. As you pass by each child they should speak aloud the thought of the character at the moment portrayed in the photo. Before doing this you might find it helpful to let each pair explain where/when, each photo was taken.

5 Collective voice/thought-tracking

Read the 'Second Voice' aloud (i.e. Smudge's father), or ask a child to read it aloud. Look with the children at the picture of Charles' mother and Smudge's father (Literacy Support Sheet 3). Divide the class into two groups. After looking at the picture, tell them that one group will speak the woman's thoughts out loud and then the other will speak the man's. Invite the members of one group at a time to speak whilst the other group listens.

> *Writing opportunity*
>
> In two headed columns, list with the children 'What the woman *knows* about the man' and 'What the woman *thinks she knows* about the man'. You might like also to draw out in discussion what the reader knows about the man that the woman does not know (with reference to the text).

6 Read the 'Fourth Voice'

> *Writing opportunity*
>
> Ask the children what they would like to know about Smudge. Ask them to write their questions to her within a large question mark (Literacy Support Sheet 4).

7 Collective voice/hot-seating

Ask the children to pretend to be Smudge. Explain that you will be asking them questions. You can use the children's own recorded questions and add others of your own. Any one of the children in turn may answer as Smudge. They will need to listen carefully to each other in order to remain consistent and convincing as one character.

8 Improvisation

Ask the children to pair up. One person will be Charles and the other will be Smudge. Tell them that it is the moment when Smudge is trying to persuade Charles to play on the slide. Let each child take it in turns to play both parts. The emphasis should be on persuasion.

9 Eavesdropping/performance carousel

The children remain in pairs as Smudge and Charles. You will pass by each pair. The children you are passing nearest to carry on enacting the scene aloud (when Smudge is persuading Charles to play). Other pairs listen as they wait their turn.

10 Decision alley

Ask the children to get into two long lines facing each other. You will walk between the lines as Charles. As you pass by, one line will give you reasons why you should go and play with Smudge and the other line will give you reasons why you should not.

> *Writing opportunity*
>
> In two columns, ask the children to list the reasons for and against going to play with Smudge. These lists can form the basis of a persuasive speech or a writing frame for structuring persuasive writing.

11 Thought-tracking

You stand in the middle of a class circle as Charles' mother at the moment she realises that Charles is missing. The children may pass by you as they change places across the circle. As they pass you by, they speak a thought out loud that is running through the mother's head.

12 Improvisation

In pairs, ask the children to improvise playing in the park as Smudge and Charles.

13 Improvisation

Charles and his mother walked home in silence but what would they have liked to say to each other? Ask the children to get into pairs (Charles and his mother). Explain that they will walk home as Charles and his mother twice. The first time they will move around the room as the walking characters in silence. The second time they will speak to each other as they would like to have spoken.

14 Improvisation

In pairs, ask the children to be Smudge and her dad walking home from the park, chatting. Afterwards encourage them to talk about the contrast/difference between this scene and the one when Charles and his mother walk home.

Writing opportunity

Create a 'Fifth Voice'. Other voices in the park can be created, orally at first maybe, and then in writing (e.g. the park-keeper, one of the dogs, a passer-by). What are their versions of events from their viewpoints?

Scriptwriting opportunity

Script a dialogue based on any of the enacted scenes between characters.

Writing opportunity

Create rules and notices for the park.

Possible assessment focus

- Were the children able to differentiate between the characters?
- Which children were able to use the drama to contribute to the writing task?
- Which children were able to create a convincing additional character (i.e. the Fifth Voice)?

Unit 4 *The Last Wolf*
by Ann Turnbull

Key Stage 1

NC year group 2

Range

Fiction: stories by significant children's authors

This story can be found in the Key Stage 1, 2000 SATs Reading Book. Where activities are directly linked to supporting children in answering specific questions from the 2000 Reading Comprehension test booklet, this is indicated in brackets.

Outline

In the past there had been many wolves roaming the countryside. The people, however, were frightened of them, so hunted and killed them until there was only one left. The King, knowing that he was the last grey wolf, put him in a cage with his own keeper and provided him with the best of everything. The wolf was unhappy. He pined for his natural home and the company of the pack. The King watched despairingly as the wolf lay still in the cage and got thinner and thinner. Everyone in the palace feared the worst and waited for the wolf to die. Then the full moon shone down and, as if by magic, created another wolf, a silver she-wolf. Grey Wolf and Silver Wolf howled together in joy and disappeared up into the hills. The King and his people vowed never to hunt the wolves again and in time the sound of howling wolves filled the night air once more.

Learning objectives

- to be aware of the difference between written and spoken language, through retelling parts of known stories
- to understand sequential relationships in story

- to identify reasons for events in stories
- to retell stories through role-play in groups, using dialogue and narrative from a text
- to use and develop a story-setting from reading through working and writing in role
- to respond imaginatively, through drama, to text
- to speculate, empathise and enact with how characters from a story might feel, think and behave

Introductory literacy activities

- Introduce and read the story to or with the children. You might wish to have different editions available to promote discussion about why there are different editions, including a SATs booklet version.
- Give groups of children the sentences below, written onto separate strips of paper. Prepare additional blank strips of paper for later use (one per child) (SATs Question 11).

The King begged the moon for help.
Grey Wolf was captured.
The moon made Silver Wolf.
The wolf cubs were born.
The King made the cage bigger.

Ask the children to put the sentence strips in sequence together. Then ask them to decide whether all the important parts of the story are covered by the sentences. Tell them that soon they will pretend to be storytellers and will be using the sentences to make sure that they do not forget the most important parts of the story, the 'key moments'. If they need a small number of additional sentences to help them remember other important parts, then each child in the group can write one extra sentence each.

This activity can be adapted as a whole class activity, rather than group activity if preferred.

Possible drama activities

1 Group storytelling

These sentences now provide the framework for a group storytelling activity. The children share out the sentence strips between them. In sequence, the group now retells the story, with each child in turn telling the part of the story for which they hold the sentence strips. The children orally add detail as storytellers. Alternatively this can be a class activity with a few children volunteering to perform as the storytellers.

2 Teacher-in-role

"The people hated wolves."

The teacher pretends to be a visitor to the kingdom who asks the children as the locals why they hate wolves. What is it about them they hate? What have they done to the people? Can they relate any incidents they have witnessed or heard of involving wolves?

Writing opportunity

Villagers can write a petition to ask the King to destroy all wolves. The reported incidents could be written as newspaper reports for an imaginary local paper or as a story written in role.

3 Dramatic game

Tell the children that they are about to hunt the last wolf. Using the same structure as the game 'What's the time Mr Wolf?' the children move in pairs around the room, one as the wolf and the other as the hunter. Whenever the wolf turns around, the hunter must stand perfectly still to avoid detection, until the wolf looks away again. This could be played as a whole class activity with one wolf and many hunters.

4 Teacher-in-role/mantle of the expert

"When the last wolf was captured the hunters brought him alive to the King. . . . He paced up and down the length of his cage and his eyes were wild."

Stand with the children in a circle, around the wolf's cage. Take the role of the King and ask the children's advice as to what will be required to make the wolf feel at home and happy in the cage (SATs Question 2). Tell them that they know more about wolves than you do. Be appreciative of their advice.

5 Working in role

Now tell them that they will be your wolf keepers and must watch the wolf carefully, ready to report back to you about how it behaves in detail. In turn, around the circle, the children as wolf keepers have the opportunity to say out loud what they can 'see' the wolf doing.

> *Writing opportunity*
>
> You could ask the children to record their collective or personal imagined wolf behaviour observations as a log.

6 Teacher-in-role/mantle of the expert

As King you visit the Keepers (wolf experts) and ask them to report back on their observations. Ask also what their thoughts and feelings about the wolf are. Why do they think he is pacing up and down? (SATs Question 3). Is he happy? What do they think the wolf is thinking and feeling? Can they justify their opinions? What new advice do they have for you?

7 Ritual/still image

The children become a variety of natural objects in the forest who are missing the wolf, e.g. tree, stream, soil, grass. The children take up different still positions in the room as the objects. As the teacher passes by each object, it speaks aloud a sentence about the missing wolf. Each sentence commences with '***Where is Grey Wolf who . . .***'. This will require careful explanation and maybe some practice, as well as possibly reading the section from the text that this relates to.

8 Teacher-in-role

Tell the children that the wolf is asleep. While he is asleep they may tiptoe into the cage one at a time and place in it some natural object brought from the forest, intended to make the wolf feel at home. They will whisper aloud what their object is, but must not wake the wolf (teacher-in-role)!

9 Hot-seating/teacher in role

"The King knew the wolf would die of loneliness."

The King (teacher) is feeling sorry for the wolf. Enlist the children's sympathy by speaking your thoughts and feelings about the lone wolf aloud (SATs Practice Question B). The children have the opportunity to talk with the King about his feelings.

> *Writing opportunity*
>
> The children write the King's thoughts and feelings at this point into a secret diary he keeps.

10 Thought-tracking

"The people gathered outside. They waited . . . The King walked out into the snow and waited."

Everyone is waiting in the snow for the moon to appear and save the wolf. Ask the children to close their eyes as there is no moonlight yet. As the teacher touches each child in turn, they will have the opportunity to say aloud what they are thinking at this key moment.

11 Guided visualisation

The children keep their eyes closed and the teacher now reads to the end of the story from 'And the moon made a wolf out of moonlight . . .'. The children try to visualise the magical scene in their mind's eye, as the teacher reads.

12 Teacher-in-role/eye-witnesses

The teacher as a blind villager, who was present but could see nothing, asks the people what exactly happened. What did they see? Where are the wolves now? Explain to the children that they should make the account as vivid and detailed as they can to help this blind person imagine it as if they saw it.

Writing opportunity

Ask the children to write eye-witness accounts of what happened in the moonlight. They can use the text to check details. The account should be written in role.

Specific assessment focus of this unit

SATs questions 2, 3, and 11 and practice question B (Reading Comprehension Test, KS1, 2000).

Possible additional assessment focus

- Which children respond imaginatively to teacher-in-role and working in role?
- Were the children able to empathise and speculate about the characters in the story?
- Which children were able to give reasons for actions and events in the story?

Unit 5 *The Man who Sold his Shadow*

Retold by Michael Rosen

Key Stage 2

NC year group 3

Range

Fiction: traditional stories

Outline

Peter is a student who works hard and is poor. One day he is invited to the home of the wealthy Mister Thomas. Peter envies Mister Thomas and wants to be rich. He is approached by a stranger, who offers to buy his shadow for a bag of gold, and Peter accepts. Many people notice that Peter has no shadow but when the parents of Mina, the woman he loves, notice, he is in trouble. Mina's father will not consent to Mina and Peter's marriage without a shadow. The stranger offers again and desperate Peter demands his shadow back in return for the gold. The stranger makes a deal for the ownership of his spirit in return for the shadow. This Peter refuses and throws the bag of gold into the river. The stranger dives into the river and disappears. Peter has lost everything, but instead of feeling despair, he experiences an unexpected peace.

Learning objectives

- to develop and portray characters, events and key incidents in a variety of ways
- to perform in groups
- to use drama to explore key moments from a text
- to respond in role, using language appropriate to a given context
- to identify turning points in a story and use freeze-frame to highlight and develop these moments
- to develop character through language and image

- to use role-play to explore moral and social issues
- to consider non-verbal aspects of communication and their impact (e.g. posture, movement)
- to write simple playscripts based on own reading and oral work and appreciate the difference between playscripts and prose
- to identify, discuss and explore main and recurring characters, evaluate their behaviour and justify their views
- to develop an existing traditional story, through drama, using the same characters and settings
- to retell main points of a story
- to discuss and empathise with characters' feelings, behaviour and relationships
- to write in role (letters, invitations, advertisements)

Introductory literacy activities

- Read the story to or with the children. Ask them to work in groups and agree and list the most important 'key' moments in the story. Each key moment should be recorded in just one sentence.
- Ask them what parts of the story are left unexplained: Who is the strange man? Why does he want shadows? What does the strange man do with the shadows?

Writing in role opportunity

We are not told why Mister Thomas invited the scholar to meet with him. Gather suggestions as to what the possible reason might be. Then ask the children to write an invitation to Mister Thomas and/or a reply from the scholar. Alternatively pair the children up, with one writing the invitation and the other replying.

Possible drama activities

1 Telephone conversation/improvisation

In pairs, seated back to back, ask them to be Mister Thomas and the scholar talking by telephone. Mister Thomas invites the scholar to meet with him and the scholar accepts. Whatever else they talk about is for the children to decide.

2 Eavesdropping

Enable the pairs to share their work afterwards by saying that you will pass by each pair in turn and 'eavesdrop' on the previous telephone conversation. It will be each pair's turn to speak when you are standing nearest to them. They will stop talking as you move away. Whilst waiting for their turn, the other children must listen to the talking pair.

3 Improvisation

In the same pairs, as Mister Thomas and scholar, Mister Thomas now takes the scholar on a guided tour of his estate and boasts his grandiose plans for the development of the property. The scholar should question Mister Thomas about his plans.

Writing opportunity

Ask the children to look at estate agents' advertisements in newspapers or agents' descriptions and to make up an advertisement and/or description for Mister Thomas's new property. They could create a 'mock up' based on a local estate agent's headed paper.

4 Collective voice/teacher-in-role

Tell the children that they are all going to be the strange man whilst you will be the scholar. They must try to persuade you to part with your shadow. Tell them that you will only part with it if they are very persuasive.

5 Decision alley

Ask them to make two long lines facing each other. You will pass between them as the scholar, Peter. As Peter passes, one line will voice reasons to him as to why he should sell his shadow. The other line will give reasons why he should not. Tell them that at the end of the lines, on the floor, is an imaginary purse of gold. If you pick it up it signals that you are selling your shadow. If you leave it where it is then you are not. Keep them in suspense (dramatic tension) before finally picking up the purse and possibly miming the removal of your shadow.

Writing opportunity

Imagine that the strange man tries to persuade Peter by letter to sell his shadow. Ask them to write his letter. Alternatively, they could devise an advertisement or poster which is aimed at persuading people to sell their shadows. Persuasive dialogue between the two characters could be used as the basis of scriptwriting short scene.

6 Thought-tracking

With the children seated in a class circle, you as the strange man, pass by each child. You have the rolled up shadow in your grasp. As you pass by each child, they are invited to speak their thoughts about the strange man with the shadow out loud.

7 Improvisation

Ask the children to either work alone or in pairs. Ask them to make themselves into a still picture, showing what they, as townspeople, might be doing on an ordinary day. At a given signal, the scene will come alive. You will pass by as Peter, and when you do so, they should respond in some way to your lack of a shadow.

8 Still image/thought-tracking

Ask the children, in groups of four, to look at the cover picture of Mina, her parents and Peter (Literacy Support Sheet 5) and then make themselves into a still image of the picture. Ask them to say a line each, in turn, that their character might have spoken, at the moment portrayed by the image. Then ask them to do the same again, but this time they will speak their character's thoughts at this moment. Draw their attention to any mismatch between what their character is saying and thinking and elicit from them possible reasons for this.

> *Scriptwriting opportunity*
>
> The spoken dialogue could be recorded and form the basis of a play script.

9 Storytelling/hot-seating

Peter makes up a lie to explain the loss of his shadow. Ask the children to each make up a lie, which Peter can tell to explain the situation. Invite children to tell different stories as Peter, explaining what has happened to his shadow. You can allow the children to cross-examine the storytelling Peter in order to elicit further details. Ask them to suggest reasons why Peter is lying and consider whether he is wrong to do so?

10 Thought-tracking/still image

Peter was 'wrapped up in his thoughts'. Ask each child to think to themselves of what one of those thoughts might have been at this point in the story. Place yourself in the centre of a class circle as Peter. Tell the children that they are all going to be Peter's thoughts and, in turn, they will have opportunity to come and wrap themselves around you (Peter). As they do so, they will speak the thought aloud. After speaking, they should hold a still shape in relation to Peter. There should be minimal or no physical contact with you. It will end with a class tableau being created, which could be brought alive with the thoughts being repeatedly voiced and you responding to them.

11 Performance carousel

Activity 10 could alternatively be done in groups of about four or five, with each group having a member as Peter. This could lead into each group performing in sequence so that everyone's devised scenes are joined into one performance piece.

12 Rumours/teacher-in-role

Ask the children to each make up something that people might be saying about Peter behind his back. They should move around whispering, spreading and gathering rumours. You could repeat this activity with you passing amongst them as Peter, allowing the opportunity to respond to you, talk to your face and/or behind your back.

13 Collective role/teacher-in-role

Ask the children to pretend together to be Peter. Tell them that you will be the strange man. They must try and persuade you to give back the shadow. In the end you will agree to do so, on condition that they all sign the bottom half of blank piece of paper (leaving room for the strange man to complete the top part afterwards in any way he chooses). Tell them that you will fill in the rest afterwards. They can trust you! Hopefully the implications of signing will become evident to the children. If not, then you may need to collect their imaginary signatures and then point out how foolish they have been in signing a document without reading it.

> *Shared writing opportunity*
>
> Ask the children in groups to draft a few sentences that the strange man might put above the signatures later.

14 Teacher-in-role/hot-seating

Next tell them that what you will write above their signatures is:

"When I die and my spirit leaves my body, the owner of this piece of paper will be able to have my spirit forever after." (Rosen 1998: 23)

Tell them that they each will have the opportunity to ask the strange man one question before he disappears. Gather suggestions about the question they might ask before being hot-seated as the man. This could be used as the basis for a questionnaire. Traditionally you are probably the devil or his messenger but you can decide for yourself who you will tell the children you are or leave it as a mystery.

15 Teacher narrator

Read aloud or tell the story from this point to the end, ensuring that you make it clear that Peter is at peace with himself now, even though he still does not have his shadow.

Writing opportunity

Ask the children, individually or in pairs, to decide upon and then write the moral of the story in just one sentence.

Possible assessment focus

- Were the children able to invent events not specified in the text?
- Were the children able to empathise with the characters' feelings and behaviour?
- Were the children able to differentiate between characters' thoughts and speech?

Unit 6 *Mufaro's Beautiful Daughters*

Retold by John Steptoe

Key Stage 2

NC year group 4

Range

Fiction: stories that raise issues (e.g. injustice) and stories from other cultures.

This African folk-tale is retold by John Steptoe (1987). His version is based on a folk-tale, which appeared in *Kaffir Folklore* (1895) by G.M. Theal.

Outline

Mufaro has two daughters, the evil and jealous Manyara and the popular and kind Nyasha. Mufaro is unaware that Manyara hates Nyasha. Nyasha is kind to all living things and befriends a garden snake, Nyoka. The King's messenger arrives and announces that the King is going to choose a wife. Manyara steals away at night in advance of her sister to increase her chance of being chosen as Queen. On her night journey she meets a hungry boy and refuses him food. She meets and ignores the advice of an old woman who tells her how to respond to the laughing trees and headless man she will soon meet on her journey.

In the morning Manyara is discovered missing from her village but her footprints are evidence that she has set off already for the city. Nyasha follows in her footsteps. She meets and feeds the hungry boy and gives sunflower seeds to the wise old woman who greets her silently and points the way. The trees bow to her and she crosses the river with her father and enters the King's city. Soon they come upon Manyara, who is distraught. She has met the King, who she says is a five-headed snake who claims to know all her faults. Nyasha enters the King's chamber and meets the garden snake, who changes back into the King. He explains that he was also the hungry boy and the old woman and therefore knows Nyasha's qualities. He proposes and wedding preparations begin. Manyara becomes a servant in the new Queen's household.

Learning objectives

- to investigate how readers respond to character
- to identify main characteristics of key characters using the information to create character actions and reactions
- to actively explore chronology in narrative and narrative order
- to use expressive and descriptive language in role to create imaginary worlds
- to identify social, moral and cultural issues in stories
- to become familiar with a story from another culture and identify themes that recur across cultures
- to explore the main issues of a story and the issues it raises for the characters
- to practise persuasive speech
- to consider and present the point of view of a character
- to use improvisation and role-play to explore and enact situations described in a text
- to interpret a text through working in role
- to develop and perform scenes through improvisation
- to use different storytelling techniques
- to draw on previous experience of drama presentation skills
- to reach agreement on drama presentation when working in a group

Introductory literacy activities

- Tell the children that the characters in the story have African names that are derived from their characteristics. Translated from the Shona language, the characters names are Mufaro (happy man), Nyasha (mercy), and Manyara (ashamed). What other words could they attribute to the main characters? What names that describe their positive and negative characteristics could they apply to themselves? What positive characteristics could they name in their friends?
- Read or tell the story to the children. Ask them if they can think of any other stories with similar themes or storylines (e.g. Cinderella).
- Brainstorm and list the universal themes of the story, i.e. 'This story is about . . .' a jealous sister, a loving and foolish father, honesty and deceit, good winning over evil and being rewarded, characters being tested on a journey, an ordinary person marrying a King, a royal disguised amongst ordinary people in order to seek and learn, people not being what they appear to be, the wisdom of the elderly, etc.
- Ask them what the moral of the story is. What lesson is the story teaching us?

Possible drama activities

1 Visioning/working in role

Ask the children to sit in a circle, close their eyes and try to imagine that they are in a small African village. What might they be able to see if they were in the village? Playing some African background music or a drumbeat may help the children engage. Tell them that in turn they have the opportunity to say '***In our village we can see . . .***' and complete the sentence, possibly adding some description (e.g. 'In our village we can see the river. It is cool and we swim in it'). This repeated opening adds a sense of ritual as a shared picture of the village setting emerges. You could pass a drum around and the person holding or beating the drum is empowered to speak. This activity can be repeated in relation to other senses (e.g. 'In our village we can hear . . . ') to guide the children to imagine multi-sensory experiences.

2 Occupational mime/improvisation

Ask the children to split into two lines that represent either side of the riverbank. Ask them to imagine that they are at the river's edge. Gather their ideas about what sort of everyday activities they would carry out as villagers by the river. Ask them to make a still image of themselves carrying out an everyday activity. Explain that at an agreed signal, such as a drumming pattern, the scene will come to life and they will improvise. At an agreed signal, the scene will freeze.

3 Occupational mime/improvisation

Now tell them that they will repeat the activity but this time the children on one riverbank will carry out their tasks as if they are Nyasha (the good) and those on the other riverbank will carry out their tasks as Manyara (the evil). Afterwards ask the children if the way they carried out the tasks was different once they became a good or evil character. If so, in what ways?

4 Communal voice/thought-tracking

Now say that you will pass by the Manyara line and then the Nyasha line, as Mufaro (their father). When you are nearest to each child it is their opportunity to say aloud what they feel, as the character, about their father.

Writing/cross-arts opportunity

We are told that Nyasha sings as she works. Ask them to write a verse of her song lyrics, or even compose and perform the song! The same song could have different lyrics written for the different sisters.

5 Communal voice/hot-seating

Cluster the children in the two sister groups with the two groups sitting and facing each other. One group remains in role together as Manyara and the other group comes out of role to ask questions of her. Tell them that they are trying to gather information about what sort of things Manyara does and says to her sister, behind her father's back. Repeat with the Nyasha group answering the other group's questions about her treatment at the hands of her sister.

> *Writing opportunity*
>
> Key information could be noted in writing by the questioning group.

> *Writing opportunity*
>
> The King's messenger proclaims that 'The Most Worthy and Beautiful Daughters in the Land are invited to appear before the King, and he will choose one to become Queen.' This could be the heading of a written proclamation for display or advertisement, with further explanation and information being created, written and maybe then proclaimed out loud in turn, by the children.

6 Teacher-in-role/improvisation

Explain that you will enter in role as the King's messenger and that the children should respond either as daughters of the village or villagers who have daughters in their families. Enter and pronounce that the King is seeking a Queen. He is inviting any worthy and beautiful girl to present herself to him. Answer questions in role and add plausible details of your own to help build the fiction.

> *Writing opportunity*
>
> Either, as a daughter, write a message or letter to the King telling him about yourself and explaining why you would be a worthy Queen or write to him on behalf of a member of your family as a parent or brother on behalf of a daughter or sister. Consider first what might constitute worthiness and what attributes a Queen might need to have.

7 Teacher-in-role/communal voice

Tell the children that they are all Manyara and you will be her father. They need to find ways to persuade you to keep Nyasha at home and only let you go to the city to meet the King (e.g. someone must stay at home to take care of the father, she can tell the King about her sister as well, etc.). How cunning can they be? This is quite challenging and you might need to let them talk amongst themselves out of role first, to share and develop their ideas before they try them out on you in role.

Writing opportunity

The persuasive arguments and schemes arising from Activity 7 could be the basis of a piece of persuasive writing in role. This could be in the form of either an anonymous note that the father receives or a signed note from Manyara to her father.

8 Decision alley

At night Manyara meets a hungry boy in the forest. Although it is unlikely that she considered feeding him, what contradictory thoughts and voices could have gone through her head before she refused and walked on? Ask the children to form two long lines facing each other with a pathway up the middle that you as Manyara will walk through. Explain that as you pass by each child, it will be their opportunity to speak aloud and try to influence Manyara. One line of children will give you reasons why you should feed the boy and the other line will give you reasons why you should not.

Writing opportunity

In two columns list the reasons for and against feeding the boy that have been voiced during Activity 8. Invite the children to add other reasons of their own. The columns can act as writing frames from which to develop a spoken and then written case for and/or against feeding the boy. The points in both columns could be used together to form the basis of a reasoned argument.

9 Tableau/speaking objects/teacher-in-role/freeze-frame

Ask the children to sit in a large class circle. Explain that they will have an opportunity to enter the circle one at a time and make themselves into a still image of a tree in the forest. Each child who enters should link themselves physically to the developing tree sculpture of bodies that is already in place. They will need to make themselves into positions that can be held comfortably for a while. Once the class forest sculpture is complete tell them that you will enter the forest as Manyara. The trees in the forest may move, laugh and speak to her as she passes. They may try to persuade you to give up the journey. They may lie to you or try to frighten you. You could repeat this activity several times allowing volunteers the experience of passing through the forest as Manyara. The activity can be tried with eyes open or closed and the different feelings evoked can be a point of discussion. The forest can be freeze-framed at intervals in response to an agreed signal.

Writing opportunity

Each child is invited to contribute one line that was or could have been spoken by a tree to Manyana as she passed by. These lines can be written on branches of a large class tree outline or on strips of paper that become branches. Alternatively the teacher can simply gather and list the sentences. The sentences can then form the basis of a piece of negotiated, shared and guided writing, which demonstrates personification.

10 Mask work

Use a cut-out face from a magazine, mounted on card, or a mask which represents the head of the headless man that Manyara passes by without speaking to. Stand somewhere in the room with the mask under your arm but facing them. Position yourself so that all children can walk past you. Tell them that you are the headless man and that they will all pass by you as if they are all Manyara. As they pass you they may speak aloud Manyara's thoughts about the headless man.

11 Storytelling/still image/performance carousel

Divide the children into five storytelling groups. Give each group one of the following sections of the story:

- The villagers discover that Manyara is missing.
- Nyasha and her father set off through the forest and meet the boy, whom she feeds.
- Nyasha and her father pass the old woman who silently signals which way they should go and Nyasha gives her sunflower seeds as a thank you.
- The trees bow down as Nyasha passes and the beautiful city comes into sight.
- They cross the river and enter the city, where they come upon Manyara who is terrified.

Ask each group to make a still image that portrays the part of the story that their sentence refers to. Each group elects a member to stand outside the still image. This child either announces the scene by reading the sentence aloud or can extend this by telling their part of the story as a narrative that accompanies the still image. Sequence their presentations of the five scenes and ask them to present their scenes and narratives in turn seamlessly, to create a collective class performance that moves the drama forward in time.

Writing opportunity

Ask each group to write a narrative section for their scene and then a group member reads the narrative aloud as their scene is presented.

12 Teacher-in-role/improvisation

Nyasha is frightened about entering the King's chamber as Manyara tells her what to expect – a five-headed snake monster. With all the children as Manyara and with you as Nyasha, give them the opportunity to describe the terrifying monster awaiting you inside the King's chamber. You can ask them questions to elicit gory details!

13 Still image/movement/freeze-frame

Ask the children to get into groups of five and to create a moving image of the five-headed snake monster. Every child needs to maintain some physical contact with the other group members as they move. Each group monster will be still until you pass by the groups in turn as Nyasha. They may make sounds as you pass but not speak. As you move away they freeze.

14 Still image/movement/freeze-frame

Repeat Activity 13 but this time as you approach each group in turn as Nyasha, group members will have the opportunity to speak to you as the snake (King) and say something good about you (e.g. 'You are kind Nyasha because you fed the hungry boy'). Give the groups time to rehearse what they will say to you when it is their turn.

Writing opportunities

- Ask the children to design and make wedding invitations.
- You could ask them to write an engagement announcement after studying some in a newspaper first.
- Write Manyara's secret diary entry which follows the engagement of her sister to the King.

Possible assessment focus

- Were the children able to use expressive and descriptive language to describe the village?
- Were the children able to speak in role about another character?
- Which children can physically portray and express the feelings of speaking objects (e.g. trees)?

Unit 7 Theseus and the Minotaur

Key Stage 2

NC year group 5

Range

Fiction: myths

This traditional Greek myth is available in many versions and the story may also be accessed via a range of Internet sites.

Outline

Theseus, son of Aegeus the ageing King of Athens, was a hero. The people of Athens were keen to welcome him home in victory, yet their celebrations were marred by a sadness and fear that hung like a black cloud over the city. An annual debt had to be paid to King Minos of Crete for a war lost by Athens and the selection and sacrifice was imminent. Seven youths and seven maidens had to be sent to King Minos of Crete to feed to the Minotaur, an awesome creature, half-man, half-beast. The horrific monster lived in the centre of a massive labyrinth, so deliberately complex and confusing that those unfortunate enough to be chosen were inevitably doomed.

Theseus, determined to rid Athens of this curse by destroying the Minotaur, volunteered to be one of these youths. King Aegeus was distraught that his beloved son had made this decision, and begged that the black sails which sped the boat to Crete would be changed to white if their homecoming was victorious.

The sea journey tested the strength and character of each individual on board, but eventually the boat moored in the harbour at Crete. The welcome was lavish, but encased in security and fear. Theseus and his companions were prisoners and the entertainment only a show to obscure their real intentions.

King Minos' daughter Ariadne had dismissed the whole event until she saw Theseus. Captured by his handsomeness and the sheer excitement of what he was about to encounter, she decided that she had to help him to achieve the impossible. With no time for niceties she met up with Theseus, showed him how to get to the centre of the labyrinth, gave him a sword and ball of string which he could unwind as he made his way in order to retrace his steps. This he did, successfully slaying the Minotaur and finding his way out of the labyrinth. Then under cover of darkness the whole group including Ariadne secretly left for Athens.

They rested on the magical island of Naxos where Ariadne became enchanted by the power of the god Dionysus. Unable to find her, Theseus left sadly for Athens. The white sails were forgotten and it was the original black ones that King Aegeus first saw on the horizon. Convinced that his son had failed he threw himself to his death into the sea.

Learning objectives

- to identify the features of myths and fantastical beasts
- to tell, write and perform their own version of a myth
- to investigate the narrative viewpoint and perspectives of heroes, villains and minor characters
- to introduce the use of chorus as an Ancient Greek theatre convention
- to make notes of a story outline as preparation for oral storytelling
- to develop scenes or incidents from a myth
- to role-play events and give views in role
- to recognise theatrical effects (e.g. sound/silence, movement/stillness)
- to mime scenes, focusing on how to convey meaning without words
- to consider ways of portraying contrasting emotions through the composition of images

Introductory literacy activities

- Look at a map of Greece (possibly using an atlas or the Internet) and identify Athens (name derived from the goddess Athena) and the Aegean Sea (name derived from King Aegeus).
- Ensure that the children understand that a myth is 'an ancient traditional story of gods or heroes which addresses a problem or concern of human existence. A myth may include an explanation of some fact or phenomenon' (National Literacy Strategy Glossary, page 83).
- Tell them the story. Ask them to give you 'emotion words' from the story that could be shown as statues.
- Draw their attention to the similarities and differences in contrasting emotions at the beginning and end of the story, i.e. victory/mourning, elation/misery. They could gather alternative groups of words for these emotions first from memory and then using a thesaurus.

Possible drama activities

1 Still image

Ask the children individually to create two contrasting still images or statues of victory/mourning or happiness/grief and repeatedly move in a controlled way between the two images.

2 Teacher-in-role

As a messenger from King Aegeus tell the children that seven young men and women from amongst them will need to be selected for sacrifice to the Minotaur.

3 Improvisation/working in role

Ask them to get into groups of four. Tell them that they are young Athenians. One person from each group will be sacrificed. They will explain to each other in turn why they personally should not be sacrificed, by justifying their personal value/importance to the Athenian community. The group can ask questions afterwards or challenge.

4 Improvisation/working in role

Ask them in their groups to come up with alternative methods of selecting/deciding who should be sacrificed. Each group will report its method in turn.

Writing in role opportunity

As young Athenians ask them to write a private letter to King Aegeus explaining why they personally should not be sacrificed. Each group could record their methods of selection and prioritise them. Alternatively their thoughts and fears about possibly being chosen could be written as a personal diary entry.

5 Tableau/still image

Theseus has returned triumphant from the war. Remind the children of the contrasting emotions mentioned earlier – victory/mourning, etc. which they showed as individual statues. Tell them that you want them to make themselves into a sculpture that shows the contrasting emotions that they worked on earlier. You may decide to show them pictures of Ancient Greek sculptures as a stimulus. At a given signal, each pair in turn adds themselves to a whole class relief freeze which is like one long continuous statue/sculpture in a line. (Such 3-D relief friezes are a feature of Ancient Greek buildings and can easily be found in reference books and on the Internet). Each person in turn could speak aloud the emotion they represent, in a manner that matches the emotion.

6 Choral speaking

Explain to the children that the Ancient Greeks used a chorus to explain what was happening in their plays and as a way of commenting on the action. The Ancient Greek style chorus below could be used for choral speaking, possibly to accompany the frieze:

We the citizens of Athens await the return of Theseus.

Hail Prince, son of Aegeus. Hail mighty conqueror. Hail hero.

We have all heard of his powerful victories, his brave and daring deeds.

We proclaim his name, his courage, his valour, supporter of the weak.

There is great sadness though. In our rejoicing, we are frightened inside.

The revenge of King Minos commits us to sacrifice every year

Seven young men and seven young women to the Minotaur.

Victory is paled by mourning and mourning by victory.

Ask them which line from the chorus best matches the frieze. Can they justify their choice?

Writing opportunity

They could create an additional chorus verse of their own, in the same style as the author.

7 Decision alley/teacher-in-role

Ask them to imagine that it is the moment when Theseus is deciding whether or not to go to the Palace of Knossos in Crete and slay the Minotaur. Ask the class to get into two long lines facing each other. You will walk between the lines as Theseus. One line will try to persuade you to go and the other will try to persuade you to stay. As you pass close to each child, it will be their turn to speak.

Writing opportunity

In two columns list the main points for and against Theseus going to Crete. This can then be used as a writing frame for persuasive writing with the children writing a secret letter to Theseus, taking either viewpoint. Alternatively, his adviser could write a balanced letter to him setting out the case for and against him leaving for Crete.

8 Teacher-in-role

After passing between the lines announce that you have decided to go and slay the Minotaur. You may wish to do this through a formal proclamation which revisits the main characters' relationships and the story so far:

> *I, Theseus, son of Aegeus, will rid Athens forever of the revenge of King Minos and the scourge of the Minotaur.*
>
> *I will lead the group of brave young Athenians and sail to Knossos, slay the Minotaur and return to you victorious.*
>
> *Wait for this, you citizens of Athens. Watch for us!*
>
> *My promise to my father, our beloved King Aegeus,*
>
> *Is that I will sail out with black sails,*
>
> *But my victorious return will be signalled by white sails!*
>
> *Watch for the white sails that show our victory.*

9 Collective voice/thought-tracking

As Theseus, you pass by each child. As you pass, they speak their own thoughts aloud after he has announced that he is going.

Writing opportunity

Each child writes their thoughts on a self-adhesive removable label, and places it around a large body outline that represents Theseus. The written thoughts could lead into diary writing the night before his departure.

10 Essence machine

Ask them all to decide on a sailing action each and an accompanying sound (e.g. hoisting sails, lifting or dropping the anchor, scrubbing decks, etc.) and to keep repeating it. They enact the action and make the sound repeatedly until you signal for them to stop.

11 Narrative

Ask them to silently repeat their sailing actions while you describe the voyage to Crete. Their actions should be adapted to fit in with your narrative. You can make a narrative of your own or use the following:

'Theseus and his people sailed for many days and nights. At times the sea was calm and still, like a great mirror of water ... At other times they were tossed, gently upon the waves. The sea played with them, swaying them gently from side to side. And there were times when they felt the power of the sea lifting them like an angry hand, tossing them up and down great white walls of wave ... And there came a day when Crete slipped slowly above the horizon and Theseus knew that his moment with the Minotaur was near ... and as he sighted land, his head was swimming with thoughts ...'

12 Freeze-frame/thought-tracking

Ask them to move slowly into one long line at the side of the boat and to look at Crete in the distance. You walk behind each person as Theseus. As you pass each child they have the opportunity to speak aloud their thoughts as they approach Crete.

Shared verse-writing opportunity

Each child can write their 'in role' thought on a strip of paper. They then get into groups of four. Each child reads their thought sentence aloud in turn and the group negotiates an agreed sequence for their four sentences. These sequenced sentences become a verse. Each group reads their four-line verse aloud. The sequence of group verses can then agreed with them and will become a class poem.

13 Still image/tableau

Working either from the imagination or preferably with suitable pictures from Ancient Greek vase paintings and statues (printed from the Internet), ask the children in small groups to make themselves into group still images depicting a scene between the time Theseus arrived on Crete and the time he entered the labyrinth.

Still image scenes could be sequenced and include:

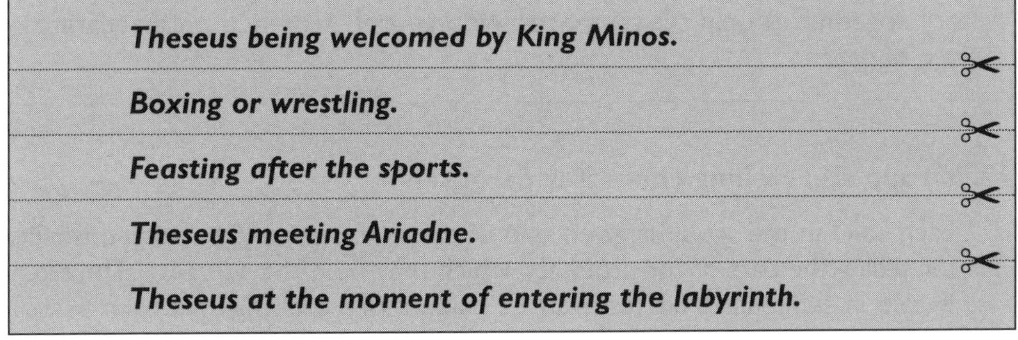

Theseus being welcomed by King Minos.
Boxing or wrestling.
Feasting after the sports.
Theseus meeting Ariadne.
Theseus at the moment of entering the labyrinth.

14 Improvisation/freeze-frame

Explain to the children, that at a given signal, their still image scenes (Activity 13) will be brought to life for a few seconds. You will then give a signal for the scene to stop. They should freeze the moment by staying perfectly still (freeze-frame).

15 Performance carousel

Ask the groups to reform their opening still image (Activity 13). Explain that you will move between each group still image in turn. When you approach a group, the scene comes to life, until you move away to the next group. Groups hold their still images until it is their turn. They remain still after you move on to the next group.

Shared group-writing opportunity

Each group could write a narrative paragraph about what is happening in their scene. The teacher can then read the paragraphs aloud in turn as each group cues for action.

16 Still image/movement

In groups of about six, ask the children to use their bodies to make part of the labyrinth. At least one person will need to keep an arm unattached, to enable each group to physically attach itself to another. This will result in all groups together collectively building one class labyrinth for the teacher 'as Theseus' to pass through. The part of the labyrinth Theseus is in at any time can move and speak and make sounds as he passes through. This can be tried again with participants' eyes closed. Several children might be given the opportunity to be Theseus passing through the labyrinth, with eyes open or closed.

Writing opportunity

Ask the children to get into groups of six. Ask them to try and write the story together in only six sentences, writing each sentence on a separate piece of paper.

17 Group storytelling/character carousel

Each child in the group is given one of the sentences and has responsibility for telling the part of the story for which they hold the sentence. The story is told in sequence. This task can be made more challenging if each person in the group tells the story from the viewpoint of a different character (e.g. Theseus, Minos, Ariadne, the Minotaur, a young Athenian, etc.). Other invented characters might include the story told by a close friend of Theseus or a palace worker.

Writing in role opportunity

After telling the story from a character's viewpoint they could write it. An alternative could be to tell the same part of the story as different characters.

18 Tableau

Tell the children that the Ancient Greeks commemorated their myths through paintings on vases, through statues, wall paintings and through relief friezes on buildings. Remind the children of the statues they formed earlier (Activity 5). Ask them to commemorate the story by each in turn making themselves into a statue portraying any moment in the story. Discourage them from all choosing the killing of the Minotaur. In turn they will each stand up and add themselves silently to a whole class relief frieze.

ICT/writing in role opportunity

Use a digital camera to photograph their relief frieze image. They could write a paragraph by a museum curator responsible for setting up an exhibition, which includes the frieze. The paragraph will explain the content and meaning of the frieze to museum visitors. They could record a commentary for blind visitors to the exhibition.

Possible assessment focus

- Were the children able to accept and identify the different features of a myth?
- Did the children understand the use of the chorus within the conventions of Ancient Greek theatre?
- Were the children able to present their views in role?
- Were the children able to use voice and movement to express different emotions?

Unit 8 *The Lady of Shalott*
by Alfred Lord Tennyson

Key Stage 2

NC year group 5/6

Range

Fiction and poetry: poetry by long-established author (narrative poetry)

This classic narrative poem by Alfred Lord Tennyson is available in an edition illustrated by Charles Keeping (Tennyson 1999). The poem can also be accessed via the Internet.

Outline

This narrative poem is in four parts:

Part 1
Downstream from Camelot is a tall, grey tower on an island. Reapers at night have heard a mysterious Lady singing in the tower and seen a light from the window, but no-one has ever seen her.

Part 2
The Lady in the tower sees the outside world reflected in her mirror. She will activate the curse that she believes is upon her if she looks directly out of her window. She weaves the reflected outdoor scenes she witnesses into her tapestry.

Part 3
The lonely Lady sees Sir Lancelot in her mirror and rushes to her window to keep him in sight. The mirror cracks when she looks out of her window and she realises that the curse has been activated.

Part 4
As if in a trance, she leaves the tower, goes to the river, writes her name on the bow of a boat, gets in to the boat and unties it and then floats up the river towards Camelot, singing mournfully and arriving at the wharf, dead. A crowd gathers and Sir Lancelot sees her and says she has a lovely face.

Learning objectives

- to describe a situation from different points of view
- to perform poems in a variety of ways
- to write from another character's point of view
- to translate, substitute and extend poetry into prose
- to understand dramatic conventions and recognise theatrical effect
- to actively empathise with a character and imagine described events
- to develop new scenes from a poem, maintaining consistency of character
- to recognise how poets manipulate words and how messages, moods and feelings are conveyed in poetry
- to increase familiarity with significant poets
- consider how meaning and impact are expressed by movement and gesture

Introductory literacy activities

- Introduce and read the poem to the children, explaining that it is a narrative poem (a poem that tells a story). It is written by a Victorian poet but is based on a medieval story, set in the time of King Arthur. You may need to explain unfamiliar vocabulary and give them access to definitions (Literacy Support Sheets 6a and 6b).
- Divide the children into four groups and allot each part of the poem to a different group. Ask each group to write the storyline for their part of the poem in as few sentences as possible. In sequence ask each group to read their part and a simple collective version of the whole storyline should emerge. Ensure that the basic storyline is understood.

Possible drama activities

Part 1 – Outside the tower

1 Movement

If you have any medieval-style music then play it first to help create the atmosphere. The children could move around to the music as if they were a person of that time or just listen.

2 Guided visualisation

Remind them that Part I describes the landscape where the story is set. Ask them to close their eyes as you read Part I again and ask them to try and visualise, in their mind's eye, a picture of the place where the poem is set.

3 Reading activity

Ask them to work with a partner, looking closely at Part I of the poem, and to underline references to things that would be 'seen' if they were present in the scene (e.g. 'long fields of barley and of rye', 'four grey walls and four grey towers', etc.).

4 Working in role

Ask them to imagine themselves now, inside the scene as one of the reapers. Invite them to offer a sentence, each in role, that describes the imaginary setting, based on what they know from the text (e.g. 'In front of me I can see fields of barley and rye waving in the wind' or 'There is a tall tower with grey walls', etc.). This activity can have a repeated opening phrase which everyone uses such as '***I can see . . .***'. You can touch the children's shoulders lightly in turn to signal their opportunity to speak.

5 Working in role

Ask them to repeat this activity, but this time they may add scenic details of their own which do not exist within the text.

Writing opportunity

Ask the children to decide in groups what they know about the Lady of Shalott from Part I of the poem and what they think they know (inference). Also what do they want to know (Literacy Support Sheet 7). Gather all their suggestions verbally. You could also list their collective ideas on an enlarged class version of the Literacy Support Sheet.

6 Working in role/still image/movement

Ask them to make a still picture of themselves as reapers at work. The version of the poem illustrated by Charles Keeping has a powerful and atmospheric picture you could use to help the children engage with their roles or you could talk briefly through what actions were involved in reaping. Once they are still, ask them at a given signal to bring the scene to life in using exaggerated, slow-motion, reaping movements. You may wish to play appropriate background music for the movement, or prefer to work in silence.

7 Teacher-in-role

Tell them that they will work in role as reapers again but that this time you will join in alongside them in as a fellow reaper who is new to the area. You will move amongst them gathering information and rumours about the lady in the tower: 'Who is she?', 'Have you seen her?', 'Does anyone live with her?' The questions you ask could include those listed previously under 'Things we want to know' (see previously suggested writing opportunity).

8 Drama game (in context)

Rumours! The children have one minute as gossipy reapers/villagers to invent, gather and create amongst themselves rumours about the Lady of Shalott.

9 Reading opportunity

You could ask them to refer back to the text afterwards in order to differentiate between those rumours that are text and non-text-based.

10 Thought-tracking

Ask the children to speak the reaper's thoughts, as they look up at the Lady's lit window at night and hear her singing. Show the Charles Keeping picture of the lit tower window if you have it and possibly play suitable singing music (medieval). They can imagine the lit tower scene if necessary, possibly building up a description of it first, before speaking their thoughts aloud about the imagined sound and image.

Part 2 – Inside and outside the tower

Introductory literacy activities

- Read Part 2 of the poem. This is set inside the Lady of Shalott's room. Check that they understand the less familiar vocabulary (Literacy Support Sheets 6a and 6b).
- Ask the children to get together with a partner and read Part 2 of the poem to themselves or each other. Ask them to work together and underline any references to scenes that the Lady has seen reflected in her mirror (e.g. 'A troop of damsels glad').
- The children could also substitute their own lines of rhyming poetry which describe other images she might have seen.

Possible drama activities

1 Improvisation/small group play-making/still image

Give the children a little rehearsal time to create a short scene depicting one of the scenes the Lady has seen (or might have seen) in her mirror. Each group should start with a still image and end with one, reinforcing the idea of the woven tapestry images of what the Lady has seen.

> *Writing opportunity*
>
> Create lines of verse to accompany scenes.

2 Performance carousel

Tell the children that you will walk slowly between each group in turn. As you pass by each group in turn, they should announce the line from the poem that they are depicting in their still image. They will then bring the still image to life until you move away, which is their signal to freeze the action. Waiting groups must remain still and silent until it is their turn. Alternatively, activate each group performance in turn with the quote 'I am half-sick of shadows'.

3 Speaking objects/working in role

Ask the children what they know, from the text, is inside the Lady's room. Ask them to also suggest what else could be there (e.g. candle, Bible, hairbrush). Ask each child to enter the drama space, which represents the Lady's room. They are each in turn invited to enter the room as any object other than the mirror, placing themselves in an appropriate position and stating what object they are. They might also add a little information about themselves in relation to the Lady (e.g. 'I am her loom. Every day she sits near me for hours').

4 Teacher-in-role/improvisation

You could walk around the imaginary room as the lady with the children speaking to you as the objects.

5 Teacher-in-role/hot-seating

Tell the children that you will now become the mirror and will answer their questions. Explain that the children will now be out of role and may ask you one question each. You will answer their questions, using your knowledge of the text. You may decide to reveal aspects of the plot that they are not yet familiar with.

6 Reading opportunity

After Activity 5, you could ask the children to work individually or in pairs, to refer back to the text and seek references linked to the mirror's answers. These could be underlined.

Part 3 – Sir Lancelot appears

Introductory literacy activities

- Read Part 3 to the children and then share out the lines or verses of Part 3 between pairs or small groups to read aloud in sequence.
- Divide the class into groups and then pair up the groups. Explain that group 1 is a 'sound group' and group 2 is a 'movement group'. Ask the sound groups to go through Part 3 underlining the direct or implied references to sound (e.g. 'And as he rode his armour rung' and 'The mirror cracked'). Ask the movement group to go through and underline textual references that refer to or imply movement (e.g. 'She left the loom' and 'Out flew the web').

Possible drama activities

1 Soundtrack/movement

Ask the sound groups to create either a sound collage or a sequence of sounds as a background soundtrack to accompany Part 3. Ask the movement group to create a short movement sequence or dance-drama linked to their underlined references.

2 Small group play-making

Now ask the groups to pair up and perform their work for each other before working together to negotiate an integrated performance incorporating aspects of both groups' work.

3 Discussion

Make sure that the children recognise the key moment in the poem, when the curse is activated. Ask them whether they think the Lady of Shalott made a conscious or unconscious decision to look directly out of the window? Can they justify their viewpoint?

4 Decision alley/teacher-in-role

Ask the children to form two long lines facing each other. Tell them that this represents the pathway the Lady followed from the mirror to the window.

You are going to move slowly between the lines as the Lady of Shalott and the children will be the contradictory voices/thoughts that could have been in her head as she moved towards the window. Each child has their opportunity to speak when you are nearest them. As you pass by one line will try and persuade you to look out of the window and the other line will try to persuade you to stop and turn back. Nobody may touch you as you pass by.

5 Teacher-in-role/thought-tracking

Move back along the lines, retracing your steps from the window. This time both lines can speak the thoughts of the Lady as she returns cursed.

6 Teacher-in-role/forum theatre

Replay the scene fast so that you do not hear or listen to the voices but rush to the window, finishing with 'The curse has come upon me'. Alternatively, the scene can be played with the children returning to their earlier roles as objects in her room (see Part 2, Activity 4). They can recreate the room and as you move towards the window they can in turn add to a commentary on the action. Which way do the children think the scene should be played to best reflect the text? Can they justify their choice? Select volunteer directors to possibly show through example how they think the scene should be played.

Writing opportunities

- Ask them to list in two columns what the two lines of children said to the Lady as she made her way to the window along the decision alley. Further possible utterances can be added.
- Write the Lady's thoughts in two columns, one listing thoughts as she approaches the window and the other as she returns cursed.
- Ask the children to draw a cracked mirror with sections. Inside each section they should write the thoughts of the Lady of Shalott at the moment the mirror cracked.

7 Teacher-in-role/hot-seating

With you in role as the Lady, invite the children to question you about this key moment in the story. You could ask groups to list questions first and restrict the number each group may ask. Ask the children to consider which of their questions are likely to elicit the most fruitful responses from the Lady.

Part 4 – The death of the Lady of Shalott

Introductory literacy activities

- Read Part 4 to and then with the children. Check that they understand the sequence of the actions of the Lady of Shalott in Part 4. List her actions together.
- Revisit the text and ask the children to consider the words Tennyson has used to describe the scene. Ask the children to suggest how he has helped us to imagine with our senses. Ask them to get into small groups. With different coloured crayons (one for each sense) ask them to underline the words and phrases that appeal to the senses (e.g. floated, singing, wind, noises of the night, singing).
- Ask them in their groups to choose one line from each part of the poem and to keep the sense of the line but to extend and elaborate it as prose, substituting words if they wish and adding others. Then they practise reading them aloud to themselves or a partner.
- Show them the John William Waterhouse painting (1888) of *The Lady of Shalott* (Literacy Support Sheet 8). Ask them to consider which aspects of the painting link directly with words or lines in Tennyson's poem (the Tate Gallery sells postcards, posters and a slide of this painting and has an online ordering service via www.tate.org.uk).

Possible drama activities

1 Movement/teacher-in-role/performance

Ask them to form two long lines a few metres apart. The space between the lines represents the river and the lines could sway to suggest the movement of the plants in the wind and the water flowing. With you in role as the Lady (teacher-in-role) silently enact her final actions in the order within the poem. Ask the children to read aloud, in turn, their extended prose lines produced during Activity 25, as you pass slowly up the river. This is a form of shared reflection. The same activity could be done more simply using a line each that they select from the poem.

2 Thought-tracking/teacher-in-role

Replay the action again and this time each child in turn has an opportunity to speak aloud a thought about the Lady of Shalott as she drifts past. Background medieval music could add atmosphere.

Lyric-writing opportunity

The Lady of Shalott sings her last song. In groups they could create the 'mournful, holy' song that she sang. These could be performed and one selected as a background to the next activity.

3 Tableau/still image

Show them the Charles Keeping illustration of the townspeople on the wharf looking at the dead body floating past (Literacy Support Sheet 9). Alternatively ask them to imagine the scene. Define where the wharf and boat are and then invite the children one at a time to enter the drama space and place themselves in the still picture entitled 'Who is this and what is here?' An atmospheric musical background could support this activity.

4 Tableau/thought-tracking

Maintain the still image and ask the children to speak aloud their thoughts in turn as they gaze upon her.

5 Teacher-in-role

You enter as Sir Lancelot and conclude the drama with the following lines:

"She has a lovely face;

God in His mercy lend her grace

The Lady of Shalott."

Writing opportunity

Ask the children to suggest how the townspeople could commemorate the Lady of Shalott (e.g. create epitaphs, write her tombstone inscription, her obituary, etc.).

Possible assessment focus

- Were the children able to negotiate in groups to create a scene, using various children's ideas?
- Which children were clearly referring to specific text when devising their scenes?
- Were the children able to use the drama to contribute to writing reflectively in role?

Unit 9 The Asrai

Key Stage 2

NC year group 6

Range

Fiction: a traditional folk-tale

This story can be found in the Key Stage 2 1997 SATs Reading Booklet for Levels 3–5. Where activities are directly linked to supporting children in answering specific questions from the 1997 Reading SATs test paper, this is indicated in brackets.

Outline

We are told that local fishermen will not fish in their nearest lake for fear of the Asrai (a potentially dangerous lake people) who may live in it. A stranger arrives in the village and decides to ignore the advice of locals and to fish in the mysterious lake. He catches fish that no-one will buy. Eventually, one night, he catches an Asrai in his nets and as he touches it he feels a burning pain. He covers the Asrai with reeds and rows ashore. On arrival, the Asrai has vanished and only a pool of water remains in the boat. The stranger's hand is now marked and he keeps it covered with a glove. At the end, the storyteller, who is wearing a glove, hints that he was the stranger.

Learning objectives

- to articulate responses in role
- to infer and deduce from text
- to develop an existing version of a folk-tale
- to develop persuasive speech
- identify dramatic ways of conveying characters and ideas and building tension
- to develop oral storytelling

Introductory literacy activities

- Introduce and read the story to or with the children, explaining that it is a folk-tale that will have been told and retold many times orally before it was written down and will have changed in the telling (SATs Question 8).
- In groups of about four, ask them to write the key parts of the story plot together in as few sentences as possible, with each sentence written on a separate strip of paper. You could challenge them to write the story in no more than eight sentences.

Possible drama activities

1 Active storytelling

These sentences now provide the framework for a group storytelling activity. The children share out the completed sentences between them. In sequence, the group now retells the story, with each child in turn telling the part of the story for which they hold the sentence prompts. The children orally add detail as storytellers. The rest of the group act out the story with the storyteller, as it is being told.

Writing opportunity

Ask the children, in pairs to locate all references to the Asrai in the text. They could underline these with a partner. Now using the headings below, gather information for the appropriate columns with the class. You may wish them to do this themselves first using Literacy Support Sheet 7, before gathering their contributions.

What we know	What we think we know	What we want to know
• People are afraid of them	• Deep, grey sad eyes • Skin sparkles • Dangerous • Rarely surface	• Do they exist?

2 Thought-tracking

"The Asrai are dangerous, even to think about."

Ask the children to be fishermen and to decide upon a secret innermost thought that they have about the Asrai in the lake. The thought can be based on the 'real' story or their own thoughts entirely. Ask the children as fishermen to move around the room, whispering, gathering and spreading their innermost thoughts to each other. At the end you gather their collective thoughts. You could spend time differentiating with them which thoughts that are directly text-based and which are not text-based.

3 Speaking objects

Ask them to sit in a class circle. Explain that they are fishermen mending their nets and thinking about the Asrai. You provide a ball of string and hold the end of the string. Explain that the string will be rolled back and forth across the circle between them all. Whoever holds the ball is empowered to speak their thoughts aloud about the Asrai before passing the string on, whilst holding a piece. By the time each child has had a turn, a visual symbol will have emerged to represent a fishing net, created by the string which they are all holding a piece of. If it is practical, leave this 'net' on the floor during the drama.

4 Working in role/shared, paired storytelling

"The lake you speak of has never been fished by our people. There are stories from the past."

The information, thoughts and feelings elicited so far can now become the starting point for creating stories about the lake. In pairs as fisherman, ask them to create and tell a story each about the lake to their partner. Partners may question to elicit further details from their storyteller.

Writing opportunity

Having created stories orally, these can now be written down.

5 Teacher-in-role/occupational mime

"Nobody would answer at first. They looked away or spoke of other things."

Tell the children that they are local fishermen, carrying out everyday fishing tasks in their village before going fishing (e.g. loading boats with nets and buckets, etc.) and you will be in role as the stranger in the story. Enter the village after setting the scene and move amongst them, asking why they will not fish in the nearest lake. As the stranger you could try to persuade or bribe the villagers to fish with you on the nearby lake, which is full of fish (SATs Question 1).

6 Teacher-in-role/occupational mime

"In the village by the lake, no-one would buy the fish that belonged to the Asrai."

Again ask the children to mime tasks as fishermen but tell them that it is now at the end of the day's fishing. Gather their task suggestions (e.g. mending nets, gutting fish, clearing boats, etc.). They have caught few fish. Enter in role as the stranger who has caught plenty in the 'mystery' lake and try to sell your fish to them. Encourage them to explain why they will not buy your fish. If necessary, ask for further explanations out of role, afterwards (SATs Question 2).

7 Freeze-frame/collective role/thought-tracking

"There seemed to be weed floating in the net, but then the young man understood . . . He had caught an Asrai."

If you have the string fishing net still available (Activity 3), gather round it with the children. If not, then make a class circle. Ask them to imagine that it is the key moment when the stranger catches the Asrai. Ask the children to make a still picture of the moment, imagining that they are all the stranger. The scene comes to life with the children speaking the fisherman's thoughts aloud as he gazes at the Asrai. You could play this scene a second time, asking the children to describe the Asrai in detail (SATs Questions 4 and 14).

> *Writing opportunity*
>
> Start with the description of the Asrai in the text and, after the drama activity, further develop the descriptions within the text by adding to it, in the same style as the author (SATs Question 14).

8 Decision alley

"In his head, the sound said, 'Let the Asrai go. Return the Asrai to the lake.' He hesitated . . ."

There is a moment of indecision suggested. Ask the children to form two long lines facing each other, with a walkway space between. Tell them that you will be walking between the lines as the young man. Ask one line of children to be the voices in his head that are telling him to throw the Asrai back. The other line, will be the voices that are persuading him to capture the Asrai. You walk up and down the lines with them speaking to you as the man's thoughts. You could finish with a mime, which suggests that you pull up the net and are scorched by pain (SATs Questions 4 and 5).

9 Hot-seating

Tell the children that you will be the young man. Sit on a chair in front of the children (preferably wearing a glove) and invite them to question you.

Try and make your answers as text-based as possible and try and find an opportunity to help them understand why you ignored the advice of the old man. Lead them into imagining what your hand looks like beneath the glove, without taking it off (SATs Questions 10, 13 and 16).

10 Mantle of the expert/teacher-in-role

Tell the children that it is many years later and the villagers want to be sure that the important messages about this incident are never forgotten. What do the old people tell the village children that they must remember from this story? Ask the children to think of one message each that they would say to a village child. Tell them that you will be the village child and go briefly to each of them in turn, as villagers. Listen to their message which they speak aloud for all to hear (SATs Question 18).

Writing opportunity

Ask the children to write their messages, the moral of the story, onto paper glove shapes and display them as a focus for shared reflection (SATs Question 18).

Specific assessment focus of this unit

SATs questions 1, 2, 4, 5, 8, 10, 13, 14, 16 and 18 (Reading Comprehension Test, 1997, KS2 Levels 3–5).

Possible additional assessment focus

- Were the children able to create descriptions of the Asrai?
- Have the children the ability to imagine and articulate the moral of the story in role?
- Were the children able to abstract sufficient information from the text about a character, to role-play and develop that character convincingly?

Unit 10 *Macbeth*

by William Shakespeare

Key Stage 2

NC year group 6

Range

Fiction: study of a Shakespeare play

Outline

1 **Macbeth as war hero**

Macbeth, Thane of Glames, is a great Scottish lord and war hero. Following a battle he is walking on a heath with his friend Banquo when they meet three witches.

2 **Macbeth's encounter with the witches**

The witches make three prophecies. Firstly, that Macbeth will become Thane of Cawdor. Secondly, he will become King and, thirdly, Banquo's sons will become Kings. Very soon the first prophecy comes true and the King, Duncan, makes Macbeth Thane of Cawdor. Duncan announces that he will visit Macbeth in his castle.

3 **Lady Macbeth's involvement**

Lady Macbeth is excited by the prophecies, which Macbeth has relayed to her by letter, and she tells Macbeth on his return home that he should murder Duncan while he sleeps.

4 **Murder of Duncan**

At first Macbeth refuses but she persuades him and he stabs Duncan in his bed. Lady Macbeth puts the blood-stained weapons in the hands of the sleeping grooms, so that they will seem guilty of the crime.

Duncan's son, Malcolm, will be his successor. Malcolm and his brother Donalbain flee for fear that they will be murdered next. The second prophecy now comes true as Macbeth is crowned King.

5 Murder of Banquo

The witches third prophecy, that Banquo's sons will become kings, obsesses Macbeth, so he hires murderers to kill Banquo and his son Fleance, but Fleance escapes. Lady Macbeth holds a banquet and Macbeth thinks he sees Banquo's bloody ghost sitting at the table.

Macbeth now believes he is being plotted against. He returns to the witches to reassure himself but his anxiety is increased as the witches imply that Macduff, Thane of Fife, is dangerous to Macbeth. However, the witches also say that Macbeth cannot be harmed by anyone who has been 'born of woman' and will be safe until Birnam Wood comes to Dunsinane. Macbeth orders the murder of Macduff's wife and five children. Macduff escapes.

6 Lady Macbeth's guilt

Guilt-ridden Lady Macbeth goes insane and dies.

7 Defeat of Macbeth, victory of Malcolm

Malcolm and Macduff lead an army recruited from England against Macbeth. They plan a surprise attack on the Castle at Dunsinane, camouflaging themselves with branches from the trees of Birnam Wood, and move towards Dunsinane. Macduff tells Macbeth that he was from his mother's womb 'untimely ripped' and Macbeth knows he is doomed. Malcolm kills Macbeth. Malcolm as the rightful heir is proclaimed King of Scotland.

Learning objectives

- to introduce a Shakespeare text
- to contribute constructively to shared discussion about literature, responding to and building on the views of others (NLS)
- to establish the themes as relevant to contemporary society
- to provide opportunities to explore language, character, setting and plot
- to experience the conventions of scriptwriting
- to compare, contrast and evaluate an Elizabethan script with a modern version
- to explore the elements of theatre
- to begin to understand Shakespeare's plays as scripts for performance
- to articulate personal responses to literature, identifying why and how a text affects a reader

Introductory literacy activities

Read or tell the children the outline of the play.

You need to ensure that the children have acquired a basic knowledge of the characters' names and relationships to each other, as well as a basic knowledge of the setting and the plot. You may use character name cards to do this (Literacy Support Sheet 10). Give out the name cards to different children to hold and as you read the outline they carry out a simple enactment of what you are saying. This makes the story immediately visual for each other and kinaesthetic for the participants. This could be done in groups or enacted by one group with the rest of the children as audience.

Ask them to get into in groups of about four and to agree and list, in sequence, the key moments:

- Macbeth as war hero
- Macbeth's encounter with the witches
- Lady Macbeth's involvement
- murder of Duncan
- murder of Banquo
- Lady Macbeth's guilt
- defeat of Macbeth, victory of Malcolm

Ask the children what they think the themes are: 'In single words, what is this play about?' List their suggestions. You may need to start them off with one or two themes. Possible themes might include:

- the supernatural
- power
- corruption
- treachery
- murder
- ambition
- guilt
- revenge
- retribution

This activity could be done in groups with the children putting themes on small strips of paper. Afterwards they each put their themes into whole class piles of their collective words. The piles will be of theme words which are the same or which have similar meanings.

Possible drama opportunities

1 Still image/freeze-frame

In groups of about four, ask them to create a still image that portrays a theme. These images may be realistic or abstract. For instance, 'Murder' could be portrayed as a realistic freeze-frame of the moment of a murder or it could be portrayed through a symbolic still image which portrays the emotions of a key character before, during and after the murder. The latter activity is more demanding.

Writing opportunities

- After reading the Shakespeare script and the modern version of Act 2 Scene 1 (Literary Support Sheet 11) aloud in groups, ask the children to compare the two versions of Act 2 Scene 1 – the discovery of Duncan's murder. Ask the children to underline anything they do not understand in both versions.
- Using two columns ask them to list the ways in which the two versions are different or similar. Which version do the children prefer? Ask them to justify their choice (possibly in writing, but verbally together first).
- Ask the children to amend, substitute or continue the modern playscript in a similar style to the playwright (more able pupils could try this with the Shakespeare text).

2 Freeze-frame/occupational mime

Tell the children that they are servants in Macbeth's castle. What might they be doing early in the morning (lighting fires, stirring porridge, polishing armour, still sleeping, etc.)? Gather their suggestions and then ask them to form themselves into a still picture (freeze-frame) as servants. Bring the scene to life and freeze it again with an agreed signal.

3 Teacher-in-role/improvisation

Tell them that it is now the moment before Macduff raises the alarm. They will bring the scene back to life but at some point you will enter as Macduff and raise the alarm about Duncan's murder. You might do this using the relevant piece of Shakespeare's text (see p. 114) or alternatively, do so in your own words. You could prime a child to ring a handbell when you finish your entry speech. The children will join with a partner or small group and improvise their immediate verbal response as servants for a while, following the discovery of the murder. Warn them in advance that they may not rush around making a loud noise in response and check that they appreciate why in relation to safety and depth of response.

"Awake! Awake! –

Ring the alarum-bell. – Murder, and treason!
Banquo, and Donalbain! Malcolm, awake!
Shake off this downy sleep, death's counterfeit;
And look on death itself! up, up, and see
The great doom's image! – Malcolm! Banquo!
As from your graves rise up, and walk like sprites,
To countenance this horror!"
(Bell rings)

4 Working in role

Ask them to select a short phrase from the above speech by Macduff or make up a line of their own, which they can move around the room saying to each other as they pass or say to themselves.

Writing opportunities

- Ask them to pretend that they are sending a short written secret message out of the castle, to a friend or member of their family, about what has happened in the castle. This could be written with lemon juice as secret ink (exposed later by the teacher or parent only by placing a candle flame under the paper).
- Alternatively the note could be written in a code of their invention.
- This task could be brought into the present day by asking them to write a text message or an email, telling of the murder of Duncan.
- A mobile phone conversation between a servant and someone outside the castle could be the basis of a section of playscripted dialogue.

5 Teacher-in-role/decision alley

The children form two lines through which the teacher as Macbeth paces as he decides as a matter of urgency what he must do about the guards. One line gives him reasons why he should kill the guards now and the other line gives him reasons why he should not.

Writing opportunity

Ask the children to write graffiti about Macbeth on the castle walls.

6 Thought-tracking

Ask the children to think to themselves what might be running through Lady Macbeth's mind as she listens to Macbeth say the following. Why does she faint? Does she really faint?

(Act 2 Scene 3)

MACBETH O! yet I do repent me of my fury,
That I did kill them.

MACDUFF Wherefore did you so?

MACBETH Who can be wise, amaz'd, temperate and furious,
Loyal and neutral, in a moment? No man:
Th' expedition of my violent love
Outrun the pauser reason. – Here lay Duncan,
His silver skin lac'd with his golden blood;
And his gash'd stabs look'd like a breach in nature
For ruin's wasteful entrance: there, the murtherers,
Steep'd in the colours of their trade, their daggers
Unmannerly breech'd with gore. Who could refrain,
That had a heart to love, and in that heart
Courage, to make's love known?

LADY MACBETH Help me hence, ho!

MACDUFF Look to the Lady.

Shared writing opportunity

Rewrite Macbeth's false speech as a true confession in Shakespearean style.

7 Hot-seating/teacher-in-role

With you in role as Lady Macbeth, invite the children to question you at this point in the story, straight after the discovery of the murder and Macbeth's speech above. You might gather their questions in advance of you taking on the role and then answer them within a soliloquy, inviting further questions afterwards.

Writing opportunity

Lady Macbeth's thoughts during and just after Macbeth's confession about the murder of the guards can form the basis of a written soliloquy.

8 Small group play-making

Divide the class into six groups and give each group one of the play extracts below.

Group 1

(Act 1 Scene 2)

For brave Macbeth (well he deserves that name),
Disdaining Fortune, with his brandish'd steel,
Which smok'd with bloody execution,
Like Valour's minion, carv'd out his passage,
Till he fac'd the slave;
Which ne'er shook hands, nor bade farewell to him,
Till he unseam'd him from the nave to th' chops,
And fix'd his head upon our battlements.

DUNCAN **O valiant cousin! worthy gentleman!**

Writing opportunities

- Retold first verbally and then in writing as an observer (e.g. one of the attendants telling a friend, or a fellow soldier).
- Retold officially by a military dispatcher.
- Presented as a spoken and/or written news report.

Group 2

(Act 1 Scene 3)

MACBETH **Speak if you can; - what are you?**

FIRST WITCH **All hail, Macbeth! Hail to thee,**
Thane of Glamis!

SECOND WITCH **All hail, Macbeth! Hail to thee,**
Thane of Cawdor!

THIRD WITCH **All hail, Macbeth! That shalt be king hereafter!**

BANQUO **Good sir, why do you start; and seem to fear**
Things that do sound so fair? – I' the name of Truth,
Are ye fantastical, or that indeed
Which outwardly ye show? My noble partner

Writing opportunities

- Retold by Banquo to his son Fleance.
- Performed as a witches spell.
- On tape as an atmospheric sound collage.

Group 3

(Act I Scene 7)

Enter Lady Macbeth

How now! what news?

LADY MACBETH **He has almost supp'd. Why have you left the chamber?**

MACBETH **Hath he ask'd for me?**

LADY MACBETH **Know you not he has?**

MACBETH **We will proceed no further in this business:**
He hath honour'd me of late; and I have bought
Golden opinions from all sorts of people,
Which would be worn now in their newest gloss,
Not cast aside so soon.

LADY MACBETH **Was the hope drunk,**
Wherein you dress'd yourself? Hath it slept since?
And wakes it now, to look so green and pale
At what it did so freely? From this time
Such I account thy love. Art thou afeard
To be the same in thine own act and valour,
As thou art in desire? Would'st thou have that
Which thou esteem'st the ornament of life,
And live a coward in thine own esteem,
Letting 'I dare not' wait upon 'I would,'
Like the poor cat i'th'adage?

MACBETH **Pr'ythee, peace.**

Writing opportunities

- Mobile telephone conversation.
- Overheard and retold by a servant.
- Diary entry by Lady Macbeth.

Group 4

(Act 3 Scene 3)

THIRD MURDERER **Hark! I hear horses.**
BANQUO ***(Within)* Give us a light there, ho!**

SECOND MURDERER **Then 'tis he; the rest**
That are within the note of expectation,
already are i'th'court.

FIRST MURDERER **His horses go about.**

THIRD MURDERER **Almost a mile; but he does usually,**
So all men do, from hence to the palace gate
Make it their walk.

SECOND MURDERER **A light, a light!**

THIRD MURDERER **'Tis he.**

FIRST MURDERER **Stand to't.**

Enter Banquo and Fleance with a torch.

SECOND MURDERER **A light, a light!**

THIRD MURDERER **'Tis he.**

FIRST MURDERER **Stand to't.**

BANQUO **It will be rain to-night.**

FIRST MURDERER **Let it come down.**

(The First Murderer strikes out the light while the others assault Banquo.)

BANQUO **O treachery! Fly, good Fleance, fly, fly, fly!**
Thou may'st revenge – O slave!

(Dies. Fleance escapes.)

THIRD MURDERER **Who did strike out the light?**

FIRST MURDERER **Was't not the way?**

Writing opportunities

- A police report.
- An obituary for Banquo.
- Retold by one of the murderers.
- Reported by Fleance.

Group 5

(Act 5 Scene 1)

(Dunsinane. A room in the Castle) Enter a Doctor of Physic and Waiting-Gentlewoman

DOCTOR I have two nights watch'd with you, but can perceive no truth in your report. When was it she last walk'd?

GENTLEWOMAN Since his Majesty went into the field, I have seen her rise from her bed, throw her night-gown upon her, unlock her closet, take forth paper, fold it, write upon't, read it, afterwards seal it, and again return to bed; yet all this while in a most fast asleep.

DOCTOR A great peturbation in nature, to receive at once the benefit of sleep, and do the effects of watching! In this slumbery agitation, besides her walking and other actual performances, what, at any time, have you heard her say?

GENTLEWOMAN That, sir, which I will not report after her.

DOCTOR You may, to me; and 'tis most meet you should.

GENTLEWOMAN Neither to you nor any one; having no witness to confirm my speech.

Enter Lady Macbeth with a taper

Lo you! here she comes! This is her very guise; and, upon my life, fast asleep. Observe her: stand close.

DOCTOR How came she by that light?

GENTLEWOMAN Why, it stood by her: she has light by her continually; 'tis her command.

DOCTOR You see, her eyes are open.

GENTLEWOMAN Ay, but their sense are shut.

DOCTOR What is it she does now? Look, how she rubs her hands.

GENTLEWOMAN It is an accustom'd action with her, to seem thus washing her hands. I have known her continue in this a quarter of an hour.

LADY MACBETH Yet here's a spot.

DOCTOR Hark! she speaks: I will set down what comes from her, to satisfy my remembrance the more strongly.

LADY MACBETH **Out, damned spot! out, I say! – One; two: why, then 'tis time to do't. – Hell is murky. – Fie, my Lord, fie! a soldier, and afeard? – What need we fear who knows it, when none can all our power to accompt? –Yet who would have thought the old man to have had so much blood in him?**

> *Writing opportunities*
>
> - Doctor's report.
> - Letter from Gentlewoman to a friend.

Group 6

(Act 5 Scene 8)

'Here may you see the tyrant.'

MACBETH **I will not yield,**
To kiss the ground before young Malcom's Feet,
And to be baited with the rabble's curse.
Though Birnam wood be come to Dunsinane,
And thou oppos'd, being of no woman born,
Yet I will try the last: before my body
I throw my warlike shield: lay on, Macduff;
And damn'd be him that first cries, 'Hold, enough!'

(Exeunt, fighting. Alarums. Re-enter fighting, and Macbeth slain.)

(Act 5 Scene 9)

Retreat. Flourish. Enter, with drum and colours, Malcolm, old Siward, Rosse, Thanes, and soldiers

SIWARD **He's worth no more:**
They say he parted well and paid his score:
And so, God be with him! - Here comes newer comfort.

Re-enter Macduff, with Macbeth's head.

MACDUFF **Hail, King! for so thou art. Behold, where stands**
Th'usurper's cursed head: the time is free.
I see thee compass'd with thy kingdom's pearl,
That speak my salutation in their minds;

Whose voices I desire aloud with mine, -
Hail, King of Scotland!

ALL **Hail, King of Scotland!** ***(Flourish)***

Writing opportunities

- From a war correspondent.
- Retold by a soldier at the scene.
- Remembered by Macduff.

Ask the groups to:

- Find their extract within a copy of the play.
- Agree together where the scene is taking place and when.
- Agree together who each character is and what they might be feeling at this point in the play.
- Agree together what is happening in the scene.

They may annotate the text as a record of their thoughts.

Writing opportunity

Add additional setting description and stage directions to the text extract.

9 Performance carousel

Once the children understand what their scene is about, ask them to select a way of presenting their scene. This could be through:

- enacting their script
- improvisation
- mime
- freeze-frame

A mixture of these strategies could be used in the same presentation (e.g. a freeze-frame that is brought alive and using selected lines of script). Sequence the group scenes and ask them to present them in a continuous sequence. Collectively they represent the key scenes in the whole play.

Writing opportunity

Write a modern version of the scenes.

Writing opportunity

Teacher and class together compose a collective narrative to link the six group presentations.

Possible assessment focus

- Were the children able to understand the plot and retell the story?
- Can the children recognise some main themes from the play and their relevance now?
- Have the children responded positively to the unfamiliar language of Shakespeare?

Part 3

Literacy Support Sheets

Introduction

The following photocopiable sheets link directly to specific units of work in Part 2 of this book. They support and extend selected activities within the units. However, teachers may consider that some of the photocopiables can be used generically.

A Royal Invitation

The King and Queen of Hearts invite

....

to attend the
Grand Royal Summer Picnic.

Date: ....

Time: ....

Place: In the palace garden.

Please reply if you would like to come

✂ ————————————————————————

I would like to come to the picnic please.

Signed ....

Palace job ....

Literacy Support Sheet 2 – Unit 2
Katie Morag and the Two Grandmothers

HOME
PRODUCE
HANDICRAFTS

BAYVIEW BARROW

© Mairi Hedderwick

Literacy Support Sheet 3 – Unit 3

Voices in the Park

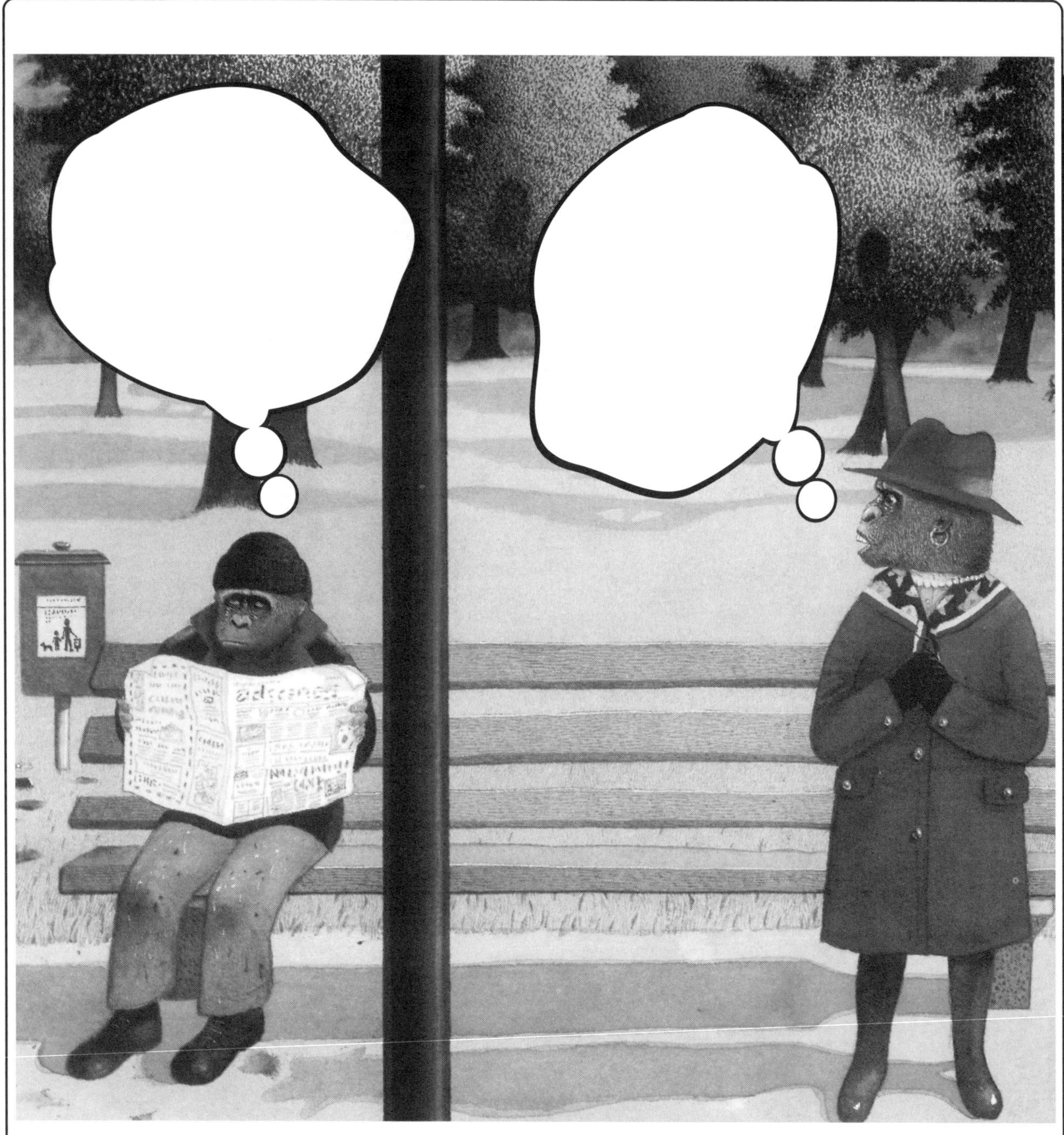

Inside the question mark, write questions that you would like to ask a character from the story.

Name of character ____________________________________

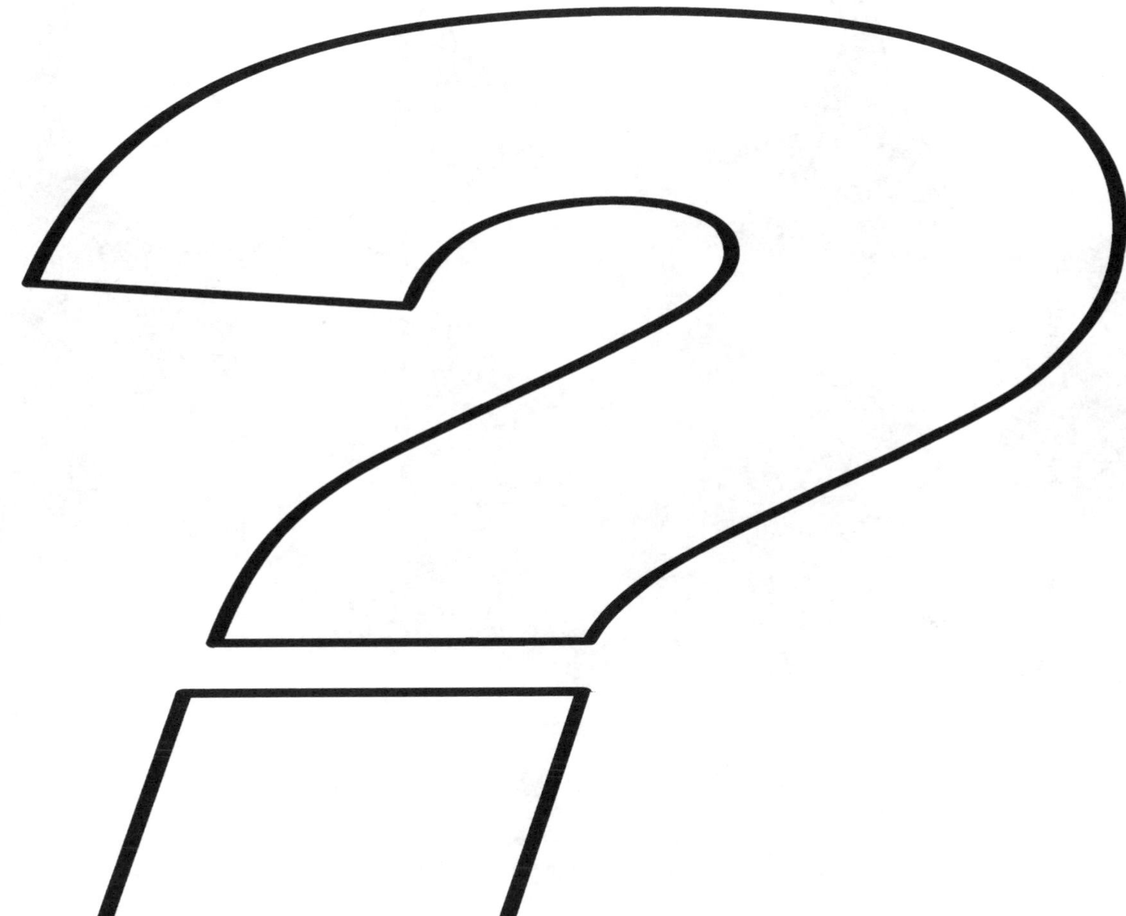

You might use different question marks:

- to put questions to different characters
- to put questions to the same character at different moments in the story.

Write what each character might be thinking.
Write what each character might be saying.

Does any character think one thing, but say something different? Why might this be?

© Illustration by Reg Cartwright.

Word and phrase definitions for 'The Lady of Shalott' in order of appearance in the text

PART 1

wold open, uncultivated countryside
meet the sky the countryside stretches to the horizon
Camelot the city in which Arthur's court meets
willows whiten the underside of willow leaves are pale and show when the wind blows
aspens a type of willow tree
dusk and shiver the surface of the water is disturbed and seems therefore darker
embowers encloses and protects as if it is closed in by a bower
by the margin the river's edge or riverbank
willow-veiled the willows are drooped like a veil, dangling in the river
shallop a light, small, open boat
casement a window

PART 2

river eddy river whirlpool currents
surly unfriendly and bad tempered
churls country people; peasants
damsels young, unmarried girls
abbot the head of an abbey of monks
pad a slow horse
page a boy who is training to be a knight
crimson deep red
plumes large, decorative feathers
lately wed recently married

Word and phrase definitions for 'The Lady of Shalott' in order of appearance in the text

PART 3

bow-shot	the distance that a bow can shoot
bower-eaves	the edge of the roof that sticks out, above her room
brazen-greaves	the armour below the knees that looked like brass
red-cross knight	a red-cross knight would be holy and represent the Church of England
gemmy bridle	the horse's bridle was covered with precious stones
Galaxy	the Milky Way
blazoned	covered with heraldic designs, a coat of arms
baldric	a belt that hangs across the shoulder and holds a sword or bugle
burnished	polished by rubbing
trode	trod
loom	a frame for weaving

PART 4

waning	getting darker
prow	the front part of a boat
seer	a person who can see into the future
mischance	bad luck
countenance	the expression on a face
carol	a song
wharfs	a landing place built at the river's edge
burgher	a citizen
mused	thought
a little space	for a short time

Word and phrase definitions for 'The Lady of Shalott' in alphabetical order

PART 1

aspens	a type of willow tree
by the margin	the river's edge or riverbank
Camelot	the city in which Arthur's court meets
casement	a window
dusk and shiver	the surface of the water is disturbed and seems therefore darker
embowers	encloses and protects as if it is closed in by a bower
meet the sky	the countryside stretches to the horizon
shallop	a light, small, open boat
willows whiten	the underside of willow leaves are pale and show when the wind blows
willow-veiled	the willows are drooped like a veil, dangling in the river
wold	open, uncultivated countryside

PART 2

abbot	the head of an abbey of monks
churls	country people; peasants
crimson	deep red
damsels	young, unmarried girls
lately wed	recently married
pad	a slow horse
page	a boy who is training to be a knight
plumes	large, decorative feathers
river eddy	river whirlpool currents
surly	unfriendly and bad tempered

Word and phrase definitions for 'The Lady of Shalott' in alphabetical order

PART 3

baldric	a belt that hangs across the shoulder and holds a sword or bugle
blazoned	covered with heraldic designs, a coat of arms
bower-eaves	the edge of the roof that sticks out, above her room
bow-shot	the distance that a bow can shoot
brazen-greaves	the armour below the knees that looked like brass
burnished	polished by rubbing
Galaxy	the Milky Way
gemmy bridle	the horse's bridle was covered with precious stones
loom	a frame for weaving
red-cross knight	a red-cross knight would be holy and represent the Church of England
trode	trod

PART 4

a little space	for a short time
burgher	a citizen
carol	a song
countenance	the expression on a face
mischance	bad luck
mused	thought
prow	the front part of a boat
seer	a person who can see into the future
waning	getting darker
wharfs	a landing place built at the river's edge

Literacy Support Sheet 7 – Unit 8
'The Lady of Shalott'

The name of the character ______________________________

The moment in the story ______________________________

What I/we ***know*** about the character	What I/we ***think we know*** about the character	What I/we ***want to know*** about the character

If you complete further copies of this sheet for the ***same*** character at different moments in the story, it will help you to see how characters develop and how your thoughts and feelings about them may change.

If you complete copies of this sheet for ***different*** characters, it is a record that helps you to compare and contrast your thoughts and feelings about different characters at various points in the story.

Literacy Support Sheet 8 – Unit 8
'The Lady of Shalott'

The Lady of Shalott by John William Waterhouse.

Literacy Support Sheet 9 – Unit 8

'The Lady of Shalott'

© Illustration by Charles Keeping, reproduced from *The Lady of Shalott* by permission of Oxford University Press.

You may wish to enlarge these character name cards before use

Duncan	**Fleance**
Malcolm	**First Witch**
Donalbain	**Second Witch**
Macbeth	**Third Witch**
Banquo	**Murderer**
Macduff	**Lady Macduff**
Gentlewoman	**Lady Macbeth**

Literacy Support Sheet 11 – Unit 10

Macbeth

Modern Version – Macbeth Act 2 Scene 1

Macduff has just left Macbeth and Lennox to go and wake King Duncan

Macduff re-enters

Macduff	Help! Help! For goodness sake someone come and help! Something horrible has happened, disgusting, tragic, hideous!
Macbeth/Lennox	What? What on earth are you screaming about? Calm down man. Get a grip on yourself. It can't be that bad. He's lost it, he's flipped!
Macduff	It is that bad, I have never seen anything like it, it's manic, it's madness. He has been murdered, there is blood everywhere. Where was the security you assured us would be here at Inverness?
Macbeth	Macduff, what are you trying to say? Who is dead?
Lennox	You can't possibly mean the King. All the security measures were activated on his arrival. Nobody could have penetrated the system.
Macduff	Well go and see for yourself. Get in that bedroom and see the horror for yourself. Don't ask me any more questions. I feel as if I am in a nightmare. Why isn't the alarm going off? Oh for heaven's sake, there has been a murder, an assassination, the King is dead. The press, they'll be here. Where's Banquo? Where are the boys? Someone, anyone, get Malcolm up and get security here now.

Exit Macbeth and Lennox. Re-enter Lady Macbeth

Lady M	What is happening? What is all this noise? People are trying to sleep, stop all this! Why is everyone up so early, and rushing about?
Macduff	Your Ladyship, I can hardly bear to tell you, indeed I can't tell you. Where is your husband? Margaret, your lady in waiting? Your personal staff? Call them, send for them.

Re-enter Banquo

Lady M	Banquo! What is going on? Where is Mac?
Macduff	The King has been assassinated Banquo. He is in the bedroom covered in blood, no pulse, it's like a horror movie, only this is real.
Lady M	The King, our guest, murdered in my house! No, no, no!
Banquo	Duffy, please just tell me that is is some kind of bizarre joke and that we can all have a drink and go back to bed. It is so early, hardly light. It can't be true! This place is recognised category 1 security. Here Mac! Len!

Re-enter Macbeth and Lennox

Macbeth	I wish I were dead too. Everything is meaningless now, quality of life has seeped away with his death, ahead only emptiness. Boys, I have bad news for you.

Enter Malcolm and Donalbain

Malcolm	Why? What has happened? Why is everyone up so early? Something is wrong? Bad news for us?
Macbeth	Yes for you and for all of us. Your Father has been assassinated. He has been stabbed to death. He never stood a chance.
Malcolm	Who did it? Where were his bodyguards? They were supposed to be with him constantly, never leaving his side. Watching him day and night. They were even sleeping in his room. His safety was high priority, you assured us Macbeth.
Donalbain	Father oh Father! What will we do?
Malcolm	Come here – hold me brother – we have to keep calm. Who is responsible for my Father's death?
Lennox	All the evidence at the moment points to his bodyguards. They too are covered in blood and the murder weapons are still lying on their beds in the room. According to Duffy the men seem traumatised, you know, out of it, in shock I should imagine, like the rest of us. Most likely extremists under cover, but who employed them? Surely they must be arrested now. Get in there and overpower them someone. Citizen's arrest that's it, before the law arrives.
Macbeth	It's too late! Sorry sorry, I couldn't stop myself. When Duffy was screaming I went to look, the scene was terrible, I will never forget it. His Majesty lying there in a pool of blood, I loved the King, I admired him, respected, even worshipped him. He was the greatest leader we have ever had, or indeed will have again. My emotion for him overcame my rational feeling and in a fit of passion I sought my revenge. Those guards will trouble us no more.
Lady M	I don't feel well! I think I am going . . .
Macduff	Quick her Ladyship is fainting. Margaret help!
Malcolm	Instinct tells me to get out of here, Don. Let's go to our room, think about what we must do and grieve for Father. Too many enemies round here, too many inconsistencies, and I can hear police sirens.
Banquo	Can you manage Margaret?

Bibliography

Browne, Anthony (1999) *Voices in the Park*, London: Corgi Books.

DfEE (1998) *The National Literacy Strategy Framework for Teaching*, London: DfEE.

DfEE (1999) *All Our Futures: Creativity, Culture and Education,* London: DfEE.

DfEE/QCA (1999a) *National Curriculum Handbook for Primary Teachers in England*, London: DfEE/QCA.

DfEE/QCA (1999b) *National Curriculum for English Programme of Study*, London: DfEE/QCA.

DfEE/QCA (2000) *The Curriculum Guidance for the Foundation Stage,* London: QCA/DfEE.

Hedderwick, Mairi (1997) *Katie Morag and the Two Grandmothers*, London: Red Fox.

HMSO (1999) 'Research Report No 115' in C. McGuinness, *Thinking Skills to Thinking Classrooms: A Review and Evaluation of Approaches for Developing Pupils' Thinking,* Belfast: HMSO.

QCA (1999) *Teaching Speaking and Listening in Key Stages 1 and 2,* London: QCA.

QCA (2001) *Planning, Teaching and Assessing the Curriculum for Pupils with Learning Difficulties in Developing Skills,* London: QCA.

Rosen, Michael (1998) *The Man Who Sold His Shadow*, Harlow: Longman.

Steptoe, John (1987) *Mufaro's Beautiful Daughters*, Harmondsworth: Puffin.

Tennyson, Alfred Lord (1999) 'The Lady of Shalott' (illustrated by Charles Keeping), Oxford: OUP.

Turnbull, Ann (1995) *The Last Wolf*, London: Hamish Hamilton.

Index